**Ooh, You Are Awful ...
But I Like You!**

Ooh, You Are Awful . . .
But I Like You!

The Life Story of Dick Emery
As Told to Fay Hillier

additional development by William Hall

SIDGWICK & JACKSON

First published 2001 by Sidgwick & Jackson
an imprint of Macmillan Publishers Ltd
25 Eccleston Place, London SW1W 9NF
Basingstoke and Oxford
Associated companies throughout the world
www.macmillan.com

ISBN 0 283 07279 2

1 3 5 7 9 8 6 4 2

A CIP catalogue record for this book is available
from the British Library.

Typeset by SX Composing DTP, Rayleigh, Essex
Printed and bound in Great Britain by
Mackays of Chatham plc, Chatham, Kent

Contents

List of Illustrations

Unless otherwise credited, photos are from the author's private collection.

In text:

Acknowledgements

To recapture the laughter and tears of Dick Emery's long and varied life would have been impossible without the wonderful help and contributions from his many friends and colleagues to all of whom I am very grateful. In order of appearance: Sergeant Frank Gray, Fred and Frank Cox, Jimmy Grafton, Sir Harry Secombe, Lionel Jeffries, Spike Milligan, Charlie Drake, John Hannam, Ronnie Barker, Clive Dunn, Michael Bentine, Lewis Gilbert, Ernest Maxim, Diana Dors, Eric Sykes, Patty Coombs, Peter Elliott, Harold Snoad, Roy Kinnear, Bert Weedon, Tony Lewis, Tony Selby, Eric Morecambe, Les Dawson, June Whitfield, Bill Cotton Jnr and John Inman.

My thanks also to Janet Coulson and Jeff Walden from the BBC. To Lew Lane, a leading authority on Music Hall. To Julia Tregellas for her good humour when asked to type the manuscript countless times as I changed my mind! In particular to William Hall without whom I would not have been able to complete this book. He taught me to write, forced me to think and provided the necessary support to see me through. And very special thanks to Margaret Thomas, Dick's devoted secretary and loyal friend, whose loving care extended to me and enriched my life.

Preface

Dick should have written this himself.

During the four years we spent together, he often talked about writing his life story. Sometimes he even got down to scribbling a few notes or a page or two, but then he would screw them up in frustration and chuck them into the bin. When he wasn't looking I rescued them, just in case he could use them later. Mostly he talked while I listened enthralled; sometimes I wrote a few notes of my own, and added them to his, hoping one day he would finally get down to writing the whole thing himself.

Sadly that was not to be.

In the last few days we spent together at our riverside home in Shepperton, Dick produced an old battered suitcase. It was crammed with photos of his life, private and professional, and of his parents' and grandparents' lives. Programmes, souvenirs and keepsakes. He said to me: 'This is my life, and I am entrusting it to you.'

During the first year after Dick's death, as a way of coping with my grief I collected every detail I could find about him, from his children, show-business colleagues and many friends, all of whom were keen to reminisce. I reread his writings and my notes, chose many photographs from his suitcase and pieced together a rough outline of his life. But it was too soon after losing him and it became too personal and painful. So I put the whole precious bundle away to await a better moment. Somehow that moment never came.

In 1999 the charity Comic Heritage honoured Dick with a blue plaque which they mounted on the wall of the BBC TV Centre at White City.

The Chairman of Comic Heritage, David Graham, asked me if I had any memorabilia on Dick and I remembered 'the book'. After so many years I was amazed to realize that no one had written a book about Dick's life, which was full of drama, and his career, which pioneered a style on TV. Encouraged by David Graham, I was determined to try to correct this oversight.

Everything I have written is as Dick told it to me or as I witnessed it first hand. I have included Dick's own words and those of his best friends and colleagues, and at last I hope it is the right moment to pay tribute to the impossible dream that was Dick Emery.

Fay Hillier

1. Early Days

'I feel a son coming on . . .'

DICK'S MOTHER

It seems inappropriate to start Dick Emery's 'own' book by talking about myself, but I feel some background is needed in order for you to understand where I'm coming from and why I figure in it.

On 3 January 1979, when Dick and I first met, I was struggling to get my career going as an actress. Having been abroad for most of my working life, it was proving difficult to get started in England. I was one of hundreds of hopefuls clutching their photos and CVs and looking for a good agent – well, any agent really.

By 1979, I had managed to get some work and had appeared on TV with Tommy Cooper, Bernie Winters and Benny Hill, so my track record was improving, but still it was an uphill struggle. I always panicked if there was nothing in my diary. So when I received the call to work on *The Dick Emery Show*, I was very pleased, even though I had no lines. Just doing background was better than nothing. At least if you were on the set, someone might notice you and give you a better part next time. Little did I know!

The make-up room at Ealing Film Studios is where I first saw Dick. I was waiting my turn to get my face done, watching the make-up girls hovering round a grubby little man who looked most unsavoury. It was, of course, Dick, dressed as one of his best-loved characters, College the Tramp, but as I wasn't particularly familiar with English TV and his disguise was very good, I didn't recognize him.

He eyed me in the mirror, clambered out of the chair and as he passed me on the way to the door, he gave me a lecherous grin that was quite revolting as most of his teeth were blacked out. As the door closed behind him, I asked the make-up girl: 'Who on earth was that?'

'That was Dick Emery,' she replied, stunned that I didn't know him. Well, it was seven o'clock in the morning and I'd been up since five. I sank into the make-up chair and concentrated on becoming glamorous.

My role was as one of the guests at a wedding reception. All I had to do was sit at a table in a low-cut evening dress while the action took place in front of me. Not too demanding. So I was surprised when the spotlight seemed to be directed at me or, to be more precise, at my cleavage. Squinting through the dazzle, I could see Dick and the lighting man giggling like a couple of schoolboys.

The day continued with several other 'funnies' from Dick in many different disguises.

At last filming ended and I headed for the exit, to find a dapper man with silver hair, a scrubbed clean face and pearly white teeth beaming at me.

This time I recognized Dick.

'Ah, there you are,' he said. 'Would you like a lift somewhere?'

'Thanks,' I replied, 'but I've got my car.'

'In that case I'll drive you to your car.'

It seemed more of a statement than a question so I fell into step beside him and we headed for his Rolls Royce. My car was only a couple of streets away, but it was much more fun to be chauffeured in a Rolls Royce. Just as I spotted my bright yellow VW Polo, Dick saw a café and made an emergency stop.

'Let's have a coffee and a chat,' he said. 'Have you got the time?'

I should have said 'No, sorry, I've got an hour's drive to get home and a family to look after,' but instead all I could manage was 'Okay'. And that's how it all began.

As we sat in the café with its Formica tables and hard chairs, I was intrigued and flattered that Dick had singled me out.

I was blissfully unaware that I fell into the stereotype of tall blonde actress that Dick usually went for, and of his reputation as a renowned flirt who looked upon a new face on set as a challenge. All I could think of was that if he liked me, he might offer me another job, hopefully with some lines. I could certainly drink a few cups of coffee if it meant getting those lines.

We chose an inconspicuous table at the very back of the small café, and I lost count of the number of coffees we drank as we talked and talked and talked.

It started with the show of course, but soon moved on to more personal things. Dick told me that he was married, but 'not very happy'. He wanted to know about my life too. I said I was also married, with two sons. I didn't add that I wasn't happy either, as it didn't seem appropriate at that moment.

We continued to chat for hours. At last the café owner turned the OPEN sign on the door to CLOSED, followed by a great deal of sighing until we got the message and vacated our seats. Dick walked me to my car.

'It's been really nice to talk to you,' he said.

'Yes, me too,' I smiled and nodded, suddenly lost for words.

'Till tomorrow then,' and he walked off with a funny little wave.

All the way home I tried to work out what was going on. Why had Dick singled me out? He had made absolutely no sexual advance, but had talked so openly and so much that one might think he was 'talk starved'. But that couldn't be. He was one of the biggest names on TV at the time. He must have hundreds of people to confide in. There seemed no logical explanation.

Next day Dick was friendly and funny and totally professional during the filming. And at the end, there he was again, waiting at the exit.

'Fancy a coffee?' he asked with a grin.

This became the pattern for the rest of the week, and I became more confused than ever. There were plenty of glamorous girls in the show, many of them younger than I was, and without the complications of children and family commitments. I wondered if he found me safer because I was more mature. I was thirty-five, although thankfully people thought I was in my twenties, which was better for getting work. Whatever the reason, I could not understand why one of Britain's top entertainment 'names' should want to spend his free time sitting in some dreary little café, drinking dreadful coffee, and pouring out his heart to a total stranger.

'Come on,' Dick insisted. 'You intrigue me. You're not the usual type

I find on my set. Tell me about your background.'

'My mother is an ornithologist and my father was a vicar, but he died when I was a child—'

'A vicar!' Dick interrupted. 'Was he anything like my vicar?'

'Certainly not,' I replied, appalled at the thought of his buck-toothed horror in a dog collar being compared to my poor father.

'All right,' Dick said hastily. 'Only joking! Now tell me where you get that posh voice from. You sound like a duchess but think like a pro. And I want to know why.'

I decided to take that as a compliment, so I told him some more. 'I was born in the Lake District where my father was a curate. After he died, Mother and I went to live with my grandmother in Bude in Cornwall. I was brought up in the oppressive conditions of a household which didn't seem to acknowledge the fact that the Victorian era had passed, which probably accounts for the posh accent, as you call it.'

Dick was fascinated. 'Go on,' he urged. 'What about your mother?'

'She spends all her time watching, writing about and drawing birds. She started the Observer series with *The Observer's Book of British Birds*.'

'You're very proud of her, aren't you?' Dick smiled. 'I'd like to meet her one day.'

I wondered if they would ever meet – and if they did, what on earth they'd make of each other, but Dick brought me back to the point by demanding: 'With a background like that, however did you get into this business?'

Reluctantly, I cast my mind back and told him the story from the beginning.

As a sickly child, I'd been sent to dancing classes to 'straighten me up'. No one expected me to fall in love with dancing or eventually to insist on a career on the stage. If they had, I'd probably have been sent to a convent. As it was, I bullied my mother into allowing me to go to stage school. The Bush Davies School in East Grinstead. There I learnt everything I could about dancing, acting and producing. Backstage, on stage and 'front of house'. I was in heaven and hooked for life.

My first job was as a dancer in pantomime at the Swansea Grand Theatre, where I was spotted by an agent for the Bluebell Girls, the famous troupe of tall dancers. At five foot eight inches I was too tall for classical ballet and was cast as a village 'boy', so it was wonderful to be enveloped in the glamorous world of the Bluebells. I was lucky enough to travel all over Europe and the Middle East until eventually I discovered the English-Speaking Theatre, based in Beirut, Lebanon, and after four years as a dancer I turned my efforts to acting and never looked back.

It was such fun taking theatre to people who otherwise wouldn't see a play for years. And when we put on a pantomime for the American Base in Saudi Arabia, it was a huge success, once they got used to a man being a dame and principal boy being a girl!

The parts kept coming until 1965 when I returned to England for a couple of years, by which time I was married and expecting my first child.

I realized I'd been chatting away for ages and stopped in embarrassment only to find Dick urging me on again.

I rattled through the last few years, and added rather ruefully that I had expected all that experience in so many plays to have counted for something in England.

'That's showbiz,' he said, and launched into the account of how he got started and what a tremendous struggle it had been for him. I was enthralled as he began his life story.

Not many people can say their life was a joke before they were even born, but Dick Emery could. On 19 February 1915, snow was drifting down in thick white flakes outside the London Palladium, on a bitterly cold night. Laurie Emery, a gifted comedian, was sitting in his dressing room backstage with his wife Bertha Callen, who was the other half of this hard-working comedy act, Callen and Emery.

They had just come offstage after doing their act, which was a fifteen-minute sketch with a complete storyline.

Suddenly, Bertha – known to all and sundry as Bert – who had been working all during her pregnancy, looked up and announced: '*I feel a son coming on!*'

Laurie rushed her to University College Hospital in Gower Street, where shortly before midnight baby Richard Gilbert Emery was born, complete with thick black hair and sideburns.

'My God,' said his father, at the first sight of his son cradled in his wife's arms. 'Isn't he ugly!'

With those choice words Dick Emery was welcomed into the world, an only child in a harsh world where his parents had no permanent home, would frequently go hungry and have no idea where the next pay cheque would come from.

Britain in those days was a bitter place for those without money, and the Emery family was, more often than not, on the wrong side of the poverty line. The Great War was being fought in foreign fields, but for a reason Dick never found out his father escaped being drafted into the trenches, and was able to stay on the less hazardous road of vaudeville.

Dick was just three weeks old when he went on tour with his parents. Callen and Emery had perfected their act, and were known in the business as a couple of supreme professionals, with their timing honed down to the last second to ride the laughs.

Bertha and Laurie had met on a touring show in South Africa. Laurie was 'second comedian', and Bertha 'second comedienne', which made them equals when it came to comedy recognition by their peers. They decided to share not only their lives but their work as well, and hired a writer named Archie Nash to write them a sketch with its own storyline that they took on tour around Britain and in variety halls across Europe.

Bertha was an Irish beauty who had been brought up in the small town of Callen in Éire. Dick could recall a childhood where he sat at his mother's knee while she wove wonderful tales of her own youth – life at a manor house, mistress of the local hunt, and other flamboyant yarns. 'She must have kissed the Blarney Stone, and I never knew how much was fact and how much was fantasy,' he would say.

What was undoubtedly fact were his mother's remarkable personality, spirit and self-discipline. In the early 1900s she toured New Zealand, which meant a six-month voyage across the globe, alone, to face an uncertain life in the theatre before audiences that, she insisted later to an open-mouthed Dick, included cannibals.

But Bertha survived the cooking pot, and came home in triumph to feature at the legendary Daly's Theatre in London's Leicester Square. The show was called *Veronique* and the producer was the formidable George Edwards, whose personal method of auditioning hopefuls was to lie down in between the seats in the last row of the stalls while the hapless 'wannabe' did his or her stuff on the stage. With no microphones in those days, the wily Mr Edwards told them: 'If I can't hear you, you don't get the job!'

As for Laurie, he made his own waves in a variety of characters and acts – he was particularly adept at using the single prop of a funny hat – and was a regular pantomime dame when Christmas came around. People in the know would say later that he was ahead of his time in comedy.

Then he met Bertha – and the double act of Callen and Emery was formed. Dick remembered it from his childhood, and in later years his mother would fill in the gaps.

The sketch began with the curtains opening to reveal Laurie onstage dressed as a bootblack, clad in a bright red coat, black trousers and a shrunken cap. His shoe stand consisted of a wooden box with *Cherry Blossom* painted on one side, and *Nugget* on the other, both of them fashionable polishes of the time. There was a footrest on the top, and a shelf for the polish at the side.

On came Bertha, dressed as a scullery maid on her day off. She was 'done up to the nines' in a dress with a split up the side that actually showed her ankles and a seductive length of calf, an outrageous outfit in those days that drew wolf whistles from all corners of the auditorium. A small hat with an ostrich feather completed the image.

She would wait for the whistles to die down, then put one foot on the box for a shine. The dialogue became 'foot and face', with Laurie enquiring: 'Where are you going to, foot?' as he slapped and scuffed away at the shoe.

'Who are you talking to, face?' the lady retorted.

And so it went on until both shoes where gleaming – by which time the scullery maid and the bootblack had fallen in love. Anxious to make an impression, he raced off to get some flowers, leaving the lady to mind the stall.

Dashing round the back of the curtain, changing as he ran, Laurie would appear seconds later from the other side of the stage dressed as a toff. The red jacket had been swapped for a tailcoat, the cap for a topper. The whole outfit was rounded off with a cloak and monocle.

The toff presents his foot for a shoeshine, and the lady has no option but to comply. While she is busy with the brushes, they chat – and, sure enough, fall in love.

'Come away with me!' the toff urges, sauntering off the stage and beckoning her to follow.

'Should I, or shouldn't I?' muses the lady, torn between her two swains. She stays onstage, singing a romantic song about the choice she has to make, giving the toff time to change back into the bootblack. Finally, she makes her decision – and runs off the stage to find the toff just as the bootblack appears from the other wings, clutching a bunch of red roses.

He sees her go, and sings a sad song of unfaithful love, weeping copious tears into the flowers.

End of sketch, down comes the curtain, and two people who became three step out to take their bow – with not a dry eye in the house!

Dick was aged four when his parents allowed him to watch their act from the stalls. When his father started the slapping and scuffing, the noise was so loud that the little lad leaped to his feet and yelled out: 'Don't hurt my mother!'

He refused to be calmed down, and the show came to a grinding halt while little Dick was led up onstage to see for himself exactly what was happening. Even then he insisted that his mother remove her shoe to make sure there was no sign of blood.

These were the days when the phrase 'music hall' had given way to 'variety' – which indeed was the name of the game and the spice of an entertainer's life. Legendary figures like Marie Lloyd, Vesta Tilley, W.C. Fields and many more had cut their teeth in our music halls – Fields, incidentally, first being billed as 'The Distinguished Comedian and Greatest Juggler on Earth, an Eccentric Tramp'. Other British comics, including Charlie Chaplin and Stan Laurel, would likewise emigrate to America to strike it rich in the early days of cinema.

But in Britain it was the speciality acts that brought in the crowds, with a magician usually topping the bill. These were the people that young Dick Emery grew up with, his 'second family' in variety theatres up and down the country. Some of those acts were inspired: Ronald Romlinson worked under the name of 'Rondart' and could hit the bullseye from ten paces, blowing darts out of his mouth.

Ninette Mongador was a juggler descended from Philip Astley, the 'father of British circus' back in 1760, with a marquee permanently sited by Westminster Bridge on the spot now covered by St Thomas'

Hospital. Gerry Lee was an animal impersonator, and known as the best pantomime cat in the business – even if he probably grew tired of being in *Dick Whittington* every Christmas.

Dick never tired of talking about the weird and wonderful people he met backstage with their amazing, if sometimes bizarre talents.

Although too young to recall the first few years of being 'on tour', Dick had vivid memories of living from day to day without a permanent home or any form of security. Just an endless succession of packing, moving on, new towns, new theatres, trudging the streets looking for accommodation, train journeys and yet more packing. He wasn't young enough to escape the diverse emotions aroused in him by his father. On one hand Dick loved him as any small child loves their dad. On the other he was terrified of his father's rough, often brutal behaviour, and yet he admired his strength and ability to hold centre stage.

One event stood out so clearly in Dick's mind that I thought he was going to cry as he told me about it

His father was immensely powerful, almost up to circus-strongman level. In shabby saloon bars in the north of England, Laurie enjoyed putting on a show 'offstage', just for an extra round of applause and maybe a couple of pints. He would demonstrate his extreme strength by making Dick stand barefoot on the palm of his hand while raising his outstretched arm to shoulder height. Dick was petrified of being dropped – but even more petrified of what would happen if he disobeyed.

'Straighten up, will you!' his father bellowed one night. 'Or I'll drop you.'

The shaking boy closed his eyes, wobbling uncontrollably. And sure enough, he finally fell – striking his head against a chair to lie on the floor stunned, but miraculously without breaking anything. His reward was a savage lashing from his father's belt, on the spot, with the blows raining down and not stopping until young Dick had wet his trousers from the pain and humiliation. Forty years later that incident would be diagnosed by a London psychiatrist as the lynchpin of Dick Emery's psychological problems.

This pathetic image and many more were branded into Dick's memory. I could see the forlorn little boy, cold and hungry on the station platform, and my heart went out to him as he continued.

'We travelled everywhere by train. I remember cold, foggy stations. It always seemed to be raining. Often we would travel on a Saturday night, as soon as Mum and Dad had finished the show. I used to get train sick, hence my loathing of trains for ever after.

'We would leave the theatre in the pouring rain, and arrive at some dimly lit station where we would wait on the platform for up to three hours, huddled together in a damp group on a bench because there was no waiting room or café for warmth and welcome.

'By now it would be the early hours of the morning, nothing moving, just the rain teeming down. Anyone will tell you that at this hour a child aged between four and eight is not at his best! I used to sing a bit, cuddled up against my mother, with my face buried deep in her coat, to keep up my spirits.

'Finally the train rumbled in, filling the sky and the station with steam. The next stage could be three hours, or maybe five. We would reach our destination before dawn, so we stayed in our carriage as the train was shunted into sidings, where we slept fitfully until the sky lightened outside the grimy windows and we stirred awake.

'Now came the problem of searching for digs, as soon as the landladies were up and about. Mum and Dad would get all our luggage and bits and pieces together, then Dad would slide the window down, open the door and jump out of the carriage onto the line. *"Come on, young 'un!"* He would grab me as I jumped after him, and lead the way across the glistening tracks to clamber onto the platform and head off into the sleeping streets.

'Where do you start? You head for the theatre, and chat up the stage doorman. Like hotel concierges around the world, they are the know-all and be-all of where to go on their patch.

'Some were good, some were bad. A bad 'un could make your week at the theatre a misery by being uninformative, unhelpful and sometimes downright rude to the bedraggled, travel-stained newcomers knocking at the Stage Door. On the other hand, a good stage doorman could make your week a wonderfully happy one.'

Dick lightened up and made me roar with laughter as he played the part of the various doormen.

'If it was going to be a good week, you'd know it the moment you stepped through the Stage Door. The clue was how clean everything was. Nothing tacky, worn or dusty. The brass doorknobs gleaming, the windows crystal clear. Everything neat and tidy.

'And we'd be greeted by a cheerful voice. "Good morning, sir and madam. I trust your journey was pleasant. What name, please? Ah yes, Callen and Emery. And I see you've got your manager with you." (Referring to me, a diminutive figure clutching my mother's hand.)

'Then Mum and Dad would get a warming cup of tea, with a glass of milk and a biscuit for me, before a carbon-copied list of boarding houses was handed to us, and we trudged out into the rain to forage for digs. It usually took two or three calls before we were accepted.

'There was a Mrs Hepplewhite, your typical seaside landlady in that she hardly drew breath, bombarding us with a verbal assault from the moment we stepped through her front door. No, she didn't mind kids . . . Will Hay was here last week . . . she'd been taking in "pro's" all her life . . .

'Hey, Mrs Hepplewhite, steady on . . .

'But she was in full flood. "Three meals a day, dears, and a can of hot water outside your bedroom door every morning to wash in . . . Be sure you're back by midnight, or you'll need a key to get in . . ." And on, and on. But they were the salt of the earth, these landladies, a legend and a law unto themselves, and they became part of the variety circus when we'd swap stories about the dragon ladies or the angels who took us under their wing and their roof.'

In the early years of his childhood, the family shared the same room – and Dick remembered the sounds of his parents' love-making as he lay in his own bed with his eyes tight shut, pretending to be asleep. 'Listening in the dark to the sounds of my mother's moans, I thought Dad was hurting her – but I was too small and too much a coward to get up and help her! I was terrified – and yet strangely jealous of her, though I can't explain why. Most nights I cried myself to sleep.

'In the morning when a tap on the door from the landlady signalled that the hot water had arrived, mother washed first, then my father, then it was my turn. I would look at my small body, then at my father stripped to the waist, and at his rippling muscles – and a sense of inferiority started to grow in me . . .'

13

These years were not as happy as they might sound for a lad who was part of an adventurous vaudeville family on the road. There was never any money to spare for luxuries or treats. Dick had no roots, no home and no real friends, and a different school every month when his parents could find one to take him in, which wasn't a foregone conclusion. The head teacher would often be unwilling to take on a boy for only a few weeks, presuming that he would be a troublemaker with nothing to lose.

More ominously, Laurie Emery's visits to local hostelries were becoming more frequent and turning into prolonged drinking bouts. The result was inevitable. Dick's father would lurch back drunk and the quarrelling would begin. Mainly it was over money, or the lack of it, and the bills that had to be paid.

Once, during a summer season at Blackpool when they had a week off, Bertha noticed her small son's only pair of shoes had holes in them. She took him into town, and bought him a smart new pair. Later that day, Laurie came back after a lengthy session in a nearby pub. Dick proudly showed off his new shoes. His father scowled. 'How much?' he demanded. Bertha showed him the receipt – and Laurie blew his top. 'Let him go barefoot!' he shouted. 'I had to when I was a kid.' And out of the room he stormed – back to the pub.

Sometimes Laurie would disappear for two weeks at a time on a drinking bout, leaving his frantic wife to wonder if she should phone the police – or sit and wait for the dreaded homecoming heralded by the slam of the front door and stumbling footsteps on the staircase.

Other times, Laurie would buy a crate of whisky, hire a taxi with a few fair-weather friends he had just met, and drive around until the whisky was finished. Bertha would get a message, usually from a street urchin who had been given a penny for his pains, and a scrawled plea on a scrap of paper: *Come and get me, I'm not well.* Whatever time of day or night, whatever the weather, she would head out into the street in search of her errant husband, bring him back and put him to bed until he was well again. At these times there was a deceptive calm – before the next storm.

Finally, enough was enough.

The flashpoint came when Dick was seven years old. The family by then was living in a small rented first-floor flat amid the sprawling streets of South London, an area where even in the early 20s back alleys looked as if they hadn't changed since the days of Dickens. Chimneys belched thick grey smoke, bare lightbulbs threw a fitful light from skeletal lamp posts, children ran barefoot on the uneven pavements, costermongers shouted their wares and horse-drawn carriages clattered through the early dawn with fish boxes from Billingsgate or sides of beef from Smithfield.

Dick knew little of this and cared less. Most days he stayed at home when his parents failed to find a school. This winter their act had 'gone quiet' with hardly a booking – there was just no work to be had.

On Christmas Eve 1922, the little boy was playing with his toys under the dining-room table when a fierce argument broke out above him, growing into a noisy shouting match that seemed to go on forever.

Finally Bertha could stand it no longer. She stopped yelling back and, suddenly dangerously quiet, spoke in a low hard voice. 'I think you'd better pack up and go, Laurie!'

He stopped too. 'What – for good?' Dick remembered the incredulity in his father's voice.

'Yes,' came the reply. 'For good.'

Strangely, Laurie did not argue. Instead, Dick – sitting transfixed on the carpet – saw a corner of the tablecloth lifted up and his father's face appear.

'Who do you want to go with, son? Your mother – or me?' Laurie Emery stared into his son's eyes.

'Mother,' Dick whispered, and pressed himself against her knees.

The tablecloth dropped back. He saw Laurie's feet turn and retreat, then heard a door open and close.

Dick did not see his father again for eight years.

2. Learning Curve

'Dick Haemorrhoids'

SCHOOL PALS

Filming on *The Dick Emery Show* was coming to an end. My undemanding part in front of the camera had been greatly overshadowed by the very demanding, sometimes harrowing experience of listening to Dick pour his heart out. The café owner had become resigned to our endless cups of coffee and chatter and no longer sighed as he turned the sign to CLOSED.

Even though Dick and I had become friends – and no more than friends – I didn't really expect him to keep in touch once we no longer had filming as an excuse to meet.

I was sure there were plenty of people only too willing to listen to him, he would move on in his glamorous world and I would settle down to the familiar routine of running my house and looking for work. The most I hoped for was that Dick would remember me when casting his next show.

Two days later I was in the kitchen of my family home in Farnham, Surrey. I had just made a large plate of sandwiches for my sons' tea, they were due home from school at any moment. The phone rang and I answered it with no expectation of hearing Dick's voice.

'Hello, it's me. Can you talk?'

'Yes.' For some reason my heart was pounding and I had to control a fit of the giggles. 'How are you?' was all I could manage.

'Missing working and missing you. Fancy a coffee?'

Here we go again, I thought, but said: 'How about tomorrow?'

'Fine. Meet me at "our café" at three o'clock.'

Click, and the phone went dead.

*

He was sitting at our usual table, hiding behind dark glasses and a copy of the *Daily Telegraph*.

'I thought you wouldn't come,' he said, 'I'm so glad to see you. Can you stand a coffee?'

'Why break the habit of a lifetime?' I smiled at him, realizing it felt as if we had known each other for years.

Dick didn't waste any time. 'Come on,' he said. 'Where were we?'

'It's your turn,' I retorted. 'Your father had just left for good.' He took up the story.

When Laurie Emery walked out on his wife and son, he took with him all the stage costumes and props, the lifeblood of their act, and what little money he could find.

A curt letter came through the door next morning from the landlord, who lived upstairs. Not knowing he was suddenly one tenant short, he was forcibly reminding them that they were several weeks behind with the rent – and had chosen Christmas Day to do it. Bertha gave young Dick his Christmas present, a toy racing car, and while the little lad happily busied himself brrm-brrm-ing it around the living-room carpet, she quietly packed their few belongings into a single suitcase, and tidied up the flat. As darkness fell, she laid the key on the kitchen table, took Dick's hand in hers, put a finger to her lips to shush him, and led him down the stairs and out into the cold night air. They never got round to paying the outstanding rent, and Dick felt uncomfortable about it every time he looked back to that time.

Bertha had enough small change for the bus ride to Hampstead where a close friend named Taffy Kelly lived. Taffy was a vibrant Welsh lady, a journalist who should have been an entertainer, and she had a rambling Victorian house looking out onto the Heath. She welcomed the forlorn pair with open arms, and when she heard the story of Laurie's defection she insisted that Bertha and Dick move in with her, to live in two attic rooms at the top of the house. 'At least this will help make it a happier Christmas for you,' she said. 'And you don't need to worry about the rent.'

But Bertha did worry. With her costumes and props gone, she made a 'big decision' – to give up show business and get a 'proper job' as a typist at one pound a week. At least it was a regular income.

As the door closed on one world it would open on another, and Bertha did her best to make a home for her young son. She used her imagination to make an elaborate game of it. The dining table was an old operating table that had been thrown out by the local hospital. Their beds were improvised from a motley collection of cases and bags, with coats as bedding, while chairs were made out of old wooden crates.

But, as Dick remembered, it was home! And in truth he had never been happier. For the first time in his life he felt settled, and as he stayed in one place he was able to make friends with the local children. Hampstead Heath was on their doorstep, and became the setting for daily war games and wild, imaginary battles. The pond by the Vale of Health was ideal for swimming and fishing, and the boys would go exploring in a whooping bunch of high excitement. They would return at the end of the day muddy, tired – and as happy as any child could be in those innocent days when the only dangers on the Heath were imaginary.

Taffy Kelly introduced them to Miss Cox, a personal friend who happened to be headmistress of a junior school up the road in Hampstead High Street. Dick was enrolled as a pupil, and settled into his first steady education with fresh enthusiasm and the urge to make up for lost time. There were just two hiccups. The school insisted that all pupils, both boys and girls, should wear silk pinafores! Dick thought this was 'sissy' and protested loudly – but to no avail. To make matters worse, someone had given his mother a second-hand pair of shoes which were just his size. Bertha made him wear them – even though they had a strap and a button and Dick was certain they were girls' shoes. He felt a right berk and got teased by the other children.

The weeks passed into months and as Dick felt more secure, he became ever closer to his mother. Almost subconsciously he found himself trying to take on his father's role, supporting Bertha emotionally and in practical ways too. He worried that whatever he could do to help was never enough. Apart from shopping and helping with odd jobs around the house, he learnt to cook, mastering dishes like omelettes, grilled fish and roast chicken. He could even make fruit pies with pastry tops. At the age of nine, the young chef would proudly present his mother with a cooked dinner that he insisted on serving up himself when she came home from work. 'Sit down, Mum. Leave it all to me!' Appreciatively and proud of her small son's expertise, Bertha did just that.

But on one hot summer evening – disaster! The young maestro had just put a pound of cherries into a saucepan to simmer when there was a yelling and whistling from the road below. 'Dick! Hey, *Dick*!' He peered out of the window. Down below a group of his friends had got hold of a football and wanted him to join in a game. Dick left the cherries and dashed down the stairs. 'Just a quick game,' he shouted, as the noisy group headed for the Heath and a makeshift soccer pitch with jackets in small piles as goalposts. Half an hour later, he remembered the cherries. 'I could smell them from across the road,' he recalled. 'Luckily the place didn't catch fire. I got a rollicking from Mum, but I suspect she didn't want to upset the chef too much.' After that, Dick always double-checked he'd turned off the stove before he went out.

Taffy Kelly had a daughter called Rosemary who was the same age as Dick. She inspired in him the first stirrings of romance, and before long he found himself praying for rainy days when they would be confined to the house and could pass the time by playing 'doctors and nurses'. Rosemary was keen to co-operate and was perhaps the first to fall under the spell of the Emery charm.

When Dick was ten, Bertha found herself a new job as a typist at a music college in Balham, with the princely take-home pay of two pounds ten shillings (two pounds fifty) a week. It meant moving house, and with great regret and a few tears, the two parted company with their attic in Taffy's home in the leafy heights of Hampstead and headed back south of the river.

Bertha had found a modest terraced house at 101 Drakefield Road, conveniently located off the busy shopping centre of Balham High Road. There was a spare room, which meant they could take in a lodger to help pay the way. The newcomer was a Miss Gale and Dick 'rather fancied' the tall, elegant woman, so much so that he hung around at the foot of the stairs just to watch her walk down. Miss Gale went in for high-heeled shoes, stockings and suspenders. Staring up from his vantage point through the banisters, Dick would get a daily eyeful of flowing skirt and sensual limbs. He admitted that he could trace his passion for stockings and suspenders back to those youthful encounters.

Inevitably, the move meant a new school for Dick. He was enrolled at St Mary's beside Tooting Bec Common, a short walk away at the end of his road, and settled in happily enough.

Though small, and forced into being something of a loner by his constant moves, he was rapidly emerging from his shell as he grew older and more confident, finding it easier to make friends with the unruly South London lads who were his new pals.

He also found a surprising new hobby that kept him engrossed for hours, and earned him extra pocket money by way of a bonus. Bertha's job left the evenings free and with a helpful nudge from her journalist friend Taffy, she had managed to get work answering letters for an agony column in a magazine. There was a backlog of scores of letters to be sorted out and replied to, both personally and in print – there was none of the 'I'm sorry, we can't enter into personal correspondence' that you get today. And as Britain's first agony aunt, Bertha felt it her duty to write to each and every one of the poor souls seeking advice. Dick, now entering his teens, was roped in to help – and gave such good advice that many of his replies were actually published.

Within weeks, Bertha became a full-time journalist in her own right. With no training, her natural writing ability carried the day, and her salary shot up to twenty pounds a week. She purchased the entire contents of a house for ten pounds – including a piano and a bike. It was classed as a 'job lot' at a local auction, and somehow no one wanted it. So Bertha snapped it up.

When Dick saw the bike leaning up against the back wall where his mother had left it, he 'went bananas' (his own words). He begged his mother to let him ride it, but Bertha took one look at the rusty machine and decided it was too unsafe. Undaunted, Dick waited until she had left the house to go shopping – and wheeled his prize new steed out through the side alley and into the road.

He had never ridden before. But this would never deter an eager young adventurer who – though he didn't know it then – had the urge for speed deeply implanted in his genes. He started pedalling, stayed upright and went round and round the block until he had the hang of it.

He ventured further afield, came to the top of a steep hill, and set off down the slope. He should have listened to his mother. Bertha was right. The bike *was* unsafe – it had no brakes. The machine hurtled down the road, wildly out of control, with its small occupant clinging on for dear life, shouting at the top of his voice. Luckily there was no traffic that morning – but there was a fence of iron railings at the foot of the hill where the road curved, and Dick went straight on.

They found him impaled on the railings – luckily only by his jacket, but hanging unconscious, with the mangled bike nearby. When he came round, Dick found half a dozen anxious passers-by tending his cuts and bruises. He was resilient enough to be able to thank them and walk slowly home – leaving the remains of the bike thrown over the fence. If Bertha noticed the absence of the bike she must have thought his battered face was punishment enough as nothing was said.

Bertha made friends easily. She had many interests and could converse knowledgeably on a wide range of subjects. People flocked to her kitchen for a cup of tea and a chat, or for a more artistic evening in the sitting room where she played the piano and led the singing in popular songs of the era. She had taught Dick to sing and he had a very good voice, but was much too shy to sing in public. At the age of five his parents had forced him onto the stage to sing with their act. He'd been so terrified, he'd never got over it.

But now, in the living room of the family home in Balham, with beer and sandwiches on the table and half a dozen new-found friends and neighbours sitting in eager anticipation, Bertha knew how to get the best out of her reluctant son. If there was one thing Dick was afraid of more than being shown up in public – it was the dark. Sitting in the corner by the fireplace, trying to look invisible, he would be summoned to the centre of the room. All eyes were upon him.

His mother would say sweetly: 'Please sing your song for us, Dick – *or go to your room!*' The small boy would plead, argue and cajole, all to no avail. Then off he would creep up the stairs and into his dark room, where there was no electricity and consequently no light. He would stay for five minutes, maybe ten – then his nerve would break and he would dash downstairs, listen for a moment outside the living-room door to his mother's melodious rendering of 'Lover Come Back', then edge inside and crouch back in his corner, hoping she had forgotten.

At the end of her number, after the applause, she would smile at him again. 'Ah, Dick, there you are. Are you ready to sing for us now?' And he was. Standing miserably next to the piano as his mother played, holding back prickling tears of embarrassment, he sang his one song, 'When the Red Red Robin', as best he could – to an enthusiastic reception that astonished him. Because the truth was that Dick had a singing voice that could have taken him into opera.

Although Dick couldn't sing in public, he was always keen and perfectly at ease playing 'theatres'. He loved to build little stages in shoeboxes, with scenery and actors cut out of cardboard. Or better still, he turned the living room into a theatre, one end was the stage with newspaper curtains hung on string. He wrote, directed and acted all the main parts, roping in the neighbourhood children for supporting roles. With a character to hide behind, Dick forgot himself and his nerves and kept his mother and her friends in stitches as they recognized the local butcher, newsagent and postman. Dick was naturally observant, picking up on little details of people's characters and exploiting them mercilessly.

With her increased earnings, Bertha decided to move Dick from the local school, where he was doing very well, to King's College, Wandsworth. He hated it. He couldn't fit in, the boys were too 'posh' and called him 'Dick Haemorrhoids' instead of Dick Emery. He stopped working at his lessons and started counting the days until he could leave.

3. Head Start

'Oi, you with the hat!'

RAILWAY PORTER

After the surprise of the first phone call, it became a regular event for the summons to 'our café', where Dick continued to pour his heart out. I got used to dropping everything, jumping into the car and dashing off to our secret meetings. I even started to turn down work if I thought it would get in the way.

After several weeks, Dick had still not made any 'improper' advances towards me. But we had formed a very strong bond of understanding and friendship. He was, of course, hugely entertaining to listen to, and reduced me to tears of laughter as easily as to tears of compassion. By now I was forming a more realistic picture of his life. He told me he was lonely, too much on his own, which he hated. Although he was surrounded by people who valued him, he felt that this was as a star not a person. And above all he was terrified that his TV series would be a flop, or that his theatre audience would hate him this time.

Initially I took this with a pinch of salt, as it was impossible to believe that such a big star couldn't live in any way he wanted. But the longer I spent in his company the more I realized how often he was in fact 'alone'. He invited me onto the set when he was filming and into his dressing room in various theatres, and although hundreds of people were milling around, no one was there *just for him*. So eventually I believed him and started to feel protective towards him – and needed myself.

We soon progressed from our café to anywhere that was convenient at the moment, and the next part of Dick's life unfolded as we were sitting on his huge motorbike in a lay-by on the Hog's Back, a lovely bit of straight road between Farnham and Guildford. Dick was living in Weybridge so it was easy for him to zoom up on his motorbike to meet me there. I'd find a parking space, don a helmet, clamber aboard and cling on for dear life as he reached 100 m.p.h., stopping at a lorry drivers' tea hut in the lay-by for a mug of strong tea and a chat. Dick adored his massive bike and pointed out all sorts of 'fascinating' details. We soon gathered a crowd of enthusiasts for bikes and for Dick, who was easily recognizable even in his leathers. He captivated his small audience by telling them a story from his childhood when he first discovered motorbikes. This story is one of the things he did actually write down himself, so here it is in Dick's own words:

As a child, my fascination for motorbikes was intense. I have a vague memory of a back yard somewhere, when I was no more than five or six years old.

In this yard was a big black motorbike that looked simply huge to me. It belonged to a young man who was lovingly taking the engine down (probably a decarb), and all the bits and pieces were lying about on the floor.

I was full of questions. 'What's this?' And: 'What's that?' The young man was very patient, and answered all my questions. Then he did something which I remember to this day as clear as if it were yesterday.

'Give me your finger!' he ordered.

Hesitantly I proffered my finger, which he gently took and inserted into the hole where the spark plug goes. Then he said: 'Feel the birdy?' And began to turn the crankshaft.

Low and behold, I felt the 'birdy' peck my finger.

For years afterwards I swore there was a 'birdy' in the cylinders of every motorbike.

Once the floodgates had opened, Dick was swept along by childhood memories and no one wanted to stop him. We soon learned that aged thirteen and already an incurable romantic, Dick lost his heart to a girl of the same age named Eileen during a holiday in the Kentish seaside town of Birchington, a few miles along the old smugglers' coast from Westgate.

'She was beautiful, she was pure, she was an angel,' Dick enthused. 'I was so smitten that I hardly dared look at her. We explored the beaches together, and I have to admit that I fell madly in love! But I was tongue-tied and could never bring myself to tell her how I really felt. I could only worship her in silence! Yet it was a wonderful summer, one I will never forget.'

Eileen was his beach playmate and they would go exploring for seashells, baby crabs and tiddlers among the seaweed-covered rocks and in the stranded pools when the tide had gone out. She gave him a photograph of herself, and young Dick treasured it for months to come, weaving his own dreams around it. They wrote once or twice, but eventually the letters stopped coming back. Eileen disappeared out of his life, and the dream of love – for the moment – faded.

At fifteen, Dick was allowed to leave school. He couldn't wait to shake the dust of King's College off his shoes, even though he had no education certificates to show a potential employer. He was free, and the world beckoned.

On the last day of his school year, Bertha sat him down in the kitchen. 'You've got to start earning a living, Dick,' she said. 'What would you like to do?'

'Dunno,' said young Dick, quite truthfully because he hadn't given such worldly matters a thought. 'I'm just glad I'm not going back.'

'Well, you've got to do *something*,' said Bertha.

'That's fine with me,' said her willing son. 'I'll do anything.'

Bertha scanned the Situations Vacant columns, and finally spotted an opening for an office boy in a City carbon-paper company. Having been accepted at his interview while wearing reasonably smart, 'normal' clothes, Bertha's theatrical instincts took over and before Dick could start his first job she insisted that he should dress for the part. She took him to a menswear shop in town, where he was fitted out with a black jacket and pin-striped trousers, complete with waistcoat and an elegant velvet-collared overcoat. An umbrella almost completed the image – and a bowler hat did the rest!

'No, not the bowler hat!' Dick pleaded. 'Must I?'

'Yes,' replied his mother, in tones that brooked no nonsense. 'You must!'

'Well, can I wear it at an angle?' That at least would show some character.

'No, it must be worn straight.'

And so the best-dressed office boy in the City of London reported for work on Monday morning – to be greeted by a storm of whistles and cheers from the other lads, and offers of 'May I take your coat, sir?' while others vigorously polished his chair with cloths until it shone.

Dick managed to muster a grin, and take it all in good part, which won him the approval of the entire office. Soon he was hitching rides on the backs of lorries to deliver messages and getting to know his way around the capital.

But the bowler hat bugged him. At the start of his second week he managed to 'lose' it, and duly reported this to his mother. 'She was absolutely furious,' Dick recalled. 'She hit the roof, gave me a lecture about responsibility and looking after things – then threw five shillings at me with orders to buy a new one from Dunn's the hatters.'

The legendary men's outfitters in Mayfair had never had such a customer in all their one hundred and twenty-year history as the small, reluctant youth who hung around on the pavement for several agonizing minutes before sidling shyly through the imposing glass doors. Dick was immediately accosted by a frosty assistant, as imposing as the premises, who enquired: 'Can I help you – sir?'

'Er – I'm looking for a hat,' Dick ventured timidly.

'What kind of hat – sir?'

'A bowler hat . . .'

Moments later Dick was being presented with a black bowler, by which time he was so unnerved that he handed over his five shillings without even trying it on, and rushed out of the shop.

It was when he tried it on and the hat come down over his eyes to rest on the bridge of this nose that he realized, too late, that it was several sizes too big. Even when stuffed with newspaper inside the brim, it still sat on his ears like a large black limpet.

The last straw, he remembered, came that same evening when he was on his way home on the Underground.

A guard on the platform was shouting to passengers to 'Move along there, pass right down inside, come on, now.' Then: 'Oi! You with the hat, move on down!' Some things in life you never forget, however hard you try, and this was one of them.

'I just froze, as every eye in the carriage turned my way. After that I took the hat to work in a paper bag to satisfy Mother – but I never wore it again.'

But the hat did bring to mind a practical joke that Dick heard about during his year in the City. A somewhat pompous and unpopular executive in a firm of stockbrokers treated himself to a brand-new bowler hat and had his initials inscribed on the inside rim. A group at the office noted the size, and went out to buy an exact replica – only a size larger. They then had his initials inserted, in exactly the same place as the original.

That evening they swapped hats. The executive donned his bowler – to find it drop over his eyes. Puzzled, he examined the interior – sure enough, there were his initials. So he lined the interior with tissue paper, until the hat fitted.

Next day, the plotters replaced the real hat, complete with a circle of tissue paper inside. That evening, sure enough, the hat sat like a pimple on the hapless victim's head.

It went on like that for a week. On the following Monday the executive failed to arrive at the office. When a phone call was made to his home, his wife answered.

'My husband has gone to the doctor,' she said. 'There's something wrong with his head!'

Dick stayed as a sartorially elegant office boy for a year. Finally, inevitably, boredom set in. He asked his mother if he could change his job – at sixteen in those days it wasn't so much 'I want' as 'May I?' Bertha understood. 'Of course you can. What do you want to try now?'

'I want to be a farmer,' Dick told her without a moment's hesitation. Adding: 'In Kent.' Memories of Eileen still lingered. By a stroke of fate Bertha did find him a job as a farm hand – and the farm turned out to be only sixteen miles from Birchington, the town where the love of his life actually lived. Dick couldn't believe his luck.

Once again, the sense of theatre inside Bertha Callen rose to the fore, and she paid handsomely to kit her only son out in plus-fours, leather boots, tweed jacket and peaked cap – more the garb of a country squire than a humble 'general hand'. Dick's arrival at the farm gates caused more mirth and merriment among the locals, but this time he genuinely didn't mind.

33

'I didn't care about getting up at four in the morning to milk the cows, about bending double for hours all day in a field "mangel-wurzeling", or tramping for miles around the fields. It was healthy, outdoor work that probably did me a lot of good – but the fact was that nothing mattered as long as I could get back to Eileen, somehow.

'I knew her address, and I borrowed a very old and unreliable bike which I'd pedal through the country roads for sixteen miles there and sixteen miles back. Young love knows no bounds. All I would do was stand in the shadows and look at her house, unable to find the courage to ring the bell. It sounds crazy, I know, but I just didn't have the bottle.

'I'd see her pull back the curtains of her upstairs bedroom and look out – and I'd dive back in case she spotted me. Sometimes she would walk out into her garden. All I had to say was: "Hi!"

'But I just couldn't bring myself to do it. Was this true love? Actually I suppose it was more like a teenage infatuation, with all the agonies that go with it.'

The agony reached a peak one night in a local pub, when Dick went out for a Friday night's drinking with the other farm hands. Between the rough and ready ribaldry and the jokes, he heard a name mentioned. A name he knew. This girl had been 'generous with her favours' to every man in the group, all of them bragging of their conquest. Her name was Eileen. And after Dick had asked a few discreet questions he realized that the wings had fallen off his, now tarnished, angel.

'I was stunned. This girl had haunted my dreams for years. Now, suddenly, there was just an empty space. I faced up to the fact: she was a tramp, nothing more. It was a dreadful lesson, and too much for me to bear. I went straight back that night, sat down and wrote a letter to my mother.

'The message was simple: *I want to come home!*'

With his heart in tatters, Dick took the train back to London and returned to his old room in the family home. His mother didn't seem too surprised to see him. 'I never thought you were cut out to be a farmer anyway, dear,' she said, putting a consoling arm around his shoulders.

But now what? Dick no longer wanted to plough the land. He tried his hand at various jobs. Washing cars in a garage for a few shillings a week. Fitting parts of the gearbox on new Bentley limousines in their factory. It was more mind-numbing than creative, but by now Bertha had developed rheumatic pains in her knees, which would grow increasingly agonizing in the next months, and was unable to work. The bills had to be paid, and there was only one provider – Dick, aged seventeen.

One day it all became too much. In the privacy of their small living room Bertha broke down and found herself pouring out all her woes to her son. Through her tears, she heard Dick's voice, resolute and reassuring. 'Don't worry, Mother. Whatever happens, from now on I'll take care of you. You need never go back to work again.'

It was a rash promise for a teenager with no training, no real job and no prospects. But Dick was almost as good as his word. From that moment until the day she died nearly fifty-five years later at the age of ninety-four, Bertha Callen did no more than six months' work.

4. Curtain Up

'Dear little Dickie'

DANCE TEACHER

People were always asking Dick what made him go into show business. He remembered his first efforts as if they were yesterday and I listened to this story many times and in many different countries around the world but never tired of hearing it.

In Australia we usually flew from one venue to the next because of the distances involved, and the Press were always waiting at the airport, hoping for an interview with Dick. Inevitably the first question would be: 'How did you get started, Dick?' No matter how bizarre the circumstances he would start to reminisce, ignoring the wind howling into his microphone, planes taking off and landing, loudspeakers booming and people interrupting with well-meaning shouts of: 'Hello there, how are you doing, Dick?' Once he got started, the crowd grew bigger and he disappeared in the throng but there was never any doubt of where he was, as bursts of laughter took turns with rapt attention.

'Mother was dead against my following the family tradition onto the stage. Probably because she remembered her own precarious youth. But one day I heard of a talent contest to be held at the Grange Cinema, Kilburn, and determined to try my luck.'

Dick decided on his costume. Plus-fours, army boots with no socks, a bow tie with no shirt and a black jacket. He wrote a short stand-up comic routine, telling stories in a Scottish accent. As he was 'hiding' behind a character he managed to overcome his nerves – and won first prize.

Bertha, who had been persuaded against her will to join the audience, had to concede that Dick was a natural comic, and promised not to stand

39

in his way if he really wanted a career on the stage. Thinking he had found instant stardom, Dick entered the next talent competition he could find. A cinema in the Edgware Road was the venue this time. But a girl who sang 'Bless This House' and reduced the audience to tears, beat him into second place. That evening Dick learnt a very useful lesson on the importance of pathos as well as humour.

Bertha now devoted all her energy into helping Dick onto the stage, not only in comic routines, but at last she persuaded him to use his naturally beautiful voice. She spent hours at the piano encouraging him to learn songs, among them a poignant little number called 'Cupid Has a Garden' and arias from popular opera where Dick could give full reign to his voice.

He went to auditions for chorus singers, and won his first professional engagement for a producer named J.D. Roberton with 'The Silver Songsters'. A month later he was prancing about the stage at the Walthamstow Palace with the 'Legionnaires', a lively troupe of fifteen boys who sang and danced for the princely sum of fifteen shillings a week.

Dick was engaged as a singer. But on the second day one of the male chorus dancers was taken ill, and Dick was summarily hauled in to fill the gap. He had to learn the whole of the tap-dance routine in one after-noon, and perform it that night – but somehow he did it, and the rest of the cast applauded the flushed and triumphant novice as the curtain fell at the end of the show.

His mother, keen to add to Dick's accomplishments, was leaving nothing to chance and decided he must now have dancing lessons. She had a few precious savings tucked away and used them to pay for him to attend classes, three times a week, at the 'academy' of one Miss Flora Haggarty, a middle-aged lady of ample proportions, who took an im-mediate shine to the small but sturdy newcomer.

'The first thing she told me was that in dancing you should be able to hold a piece of toilet tissue between you and it wouldn't fall to the ground,' Dick recalled, with a wry smile at the memory of being clutched in a potentially lethal embrace by his statuesque tutor.

'When she held me, my head disappeared up her cleavage, and I could only hear part of her instructions because I had a heaving bosom pressed

40

to each ear! I have to say that as a teenager I rather enjoyed learning to dance.'

Dick's next engagement was in the chorus at the Empire Theatre, Bootle, starring comedian Ben Warris and the tap-dancing Coal Brothers, and featuring an enormous number of cockroaches!

Dick always came out in goosebumps when he got to this part of the story.

'I could smell them! The theatre was overrun with them. No matter how many times they were fumigated, they always seemed to come back in ever-increasing numbers. I'd walk in – one sniff round and I knew they were there! Sometimes they'd be vanishing down a hole in the skirting board. Worst of all was when they'd actually drop on your head from above when you were onstage – it happened to me more than once, and I tell you, it took a lot of self-control not to shout: "*Yaaagh!*" and rush from the stage.'

Using his newly acquired dancing skills, the now eighteen-year-old Dick got a job in a variety show touring the UK. He was in the chorus that was made up of twelve boys and twelve girls who shared two single-sex dressing rooms. Dick soon discovered that apart from him they might as well have all shared the same room, but once he had made it clear he was 'straight' he found he had nothing to worry about.

'The boys' even protected him from their visiting friends. 'She's not one of us,' they would say. 'She's a bona chick.' They were great fun and Dick loved them all, platonically.

He recalled: 'The boys wore fantastic make-up for the shows. It was before the days of roll-on mascara, and the eye make-up they wore was called "hot black". This meant it had to be melted over a candle and applied to their lashes before it could set. Highly dangerous, I thought. But they'd got it down to a fine art, and I was just fascinated by watching them every night and seeing the little black blobs that would form on the end of each lash.

'It beat me how they managed to keep their eyes open under all that weight!'

But they did, and the backstage shenanigans were an eye-opener too, in every sense!

Dick recalled with a grin: 'There were two performances each night, with time off in between. The boys used their free time to put on their own shows backstage, creating lavish drag costumes that the public would never see, with wonderful wigs and loads of sequins, feathers and ribbons with which they used to festoon themselves.

'I was so fascinated by their characters, mannerisms and speech, that I subconsciously stored it all away in my memory, to be brought out years later for my "Honky Tonk" character, or Clarence, to give him his proper name, whose catch-phrase was: "Hello, Honky Tonks, how are you?" He embodied the good-natured fun, the flamboyant taste in clothes and the "camp" behaviour that I had witnessed first hand.'

By the time Dick reached his nineteenth birthday he had gained quite a lot of professional experience onstage. But this was not enough for ambitious Bertha, who still thought her son could do more with his voice. She was determined to find him an operatic tutor in London, and regardless of the cost she enrolled him with the Italian tenor Cecco Mattannia. Dick was willing to learn as much as he could but the problem was paying for it. In order to earn he had to work, but the available work was always on tour out of London – Dick had to find some other job in London, and so be available for his lessons.

Dick's love of machines was not confined to cycles and motorbikes. He also loved cars. Not that he owned one, but he had driven a friend's and so he thought it quite reasonable to present himself at the Central Motor Institute in Finchley Road, North London, where he was given a test to become a driving instructor. He passed, and started work.

His fee was one shilling for every half-hour lesson, and Dick said that he earned every penny of it.

'Pupil one was a nervous lady who became hysterical in moments of crisis and forgot to use the foot brake. An old-age pensioner suddenly stepped into the road, and while I was shouting "Brake! *Brake!*" she was hammering furiously on the window, shouting even louder: "*Get out of the road, you old fool!*" Years later she became part of my Duchess character.

'Pupil two was a gentleman of middle age and cheery disposition. I walked out to the car from the driving centre with him, when I suddenly realized something. He was on crutches! Looking more closely, I saw that he only had one leg! Well, I thought, if he's up for it, so am I.

'It became a special challenge. The only way to keep him and the car on the road was to teach him a form of tap dancing on the pedals. Fred Astaire had nothing on that man! Amazingly, he got the hang of it in half a dozen lessons, and passed his test within a month. I think things were possibly a little more relaxed in those days.

'Pupil three was the man I admired most, even more than my one-legged hero. Philip was deaf and dumb. All the lessons had to be written down, which meant I got through pad after pad of notepaper and waved the pages in front of him while he was driving. *Turn right! Left hand down! Foot on the clutch when you brake!* It sounds terribly dangerous, doesn't it? But somehow it worked.

'Philip had a girlfriend – who was also deaf and dumb. She would sit in the back seat, and do sign language into the rear-view mirror. Can you imagine it? Yet somehow Philip got through too, and invited me out for a drive to celebrate passing his test.

'I sat with him in the front, and remember that a sports car shot past us on the main road, very close and unexpected, and when he'd finished braking Philip turned to me and mouthed: *"Bollocks!"* By then I'd learned to read his lips, so I could nod back: *"Yes!"*

The singing lessons continued for three years with the driving instruction to pay for them, during which time Dick stored away a huge variety of characters and ridiculous situations for future reference.

Cecco Mattannia was delighted with his pupil. Dick's voice was strengthening all the time. If only he could learn to control his nerves there was a bright future for him. In 1938, Signor Cecco informed Dick that he was ready to move onto a new teacher. He recommended the famous Luisa Tetrazzini, who coached exceptional students at her home in Milan, Italy. Dick opened his mouth to say he couldn't afford it but the signor cut him off: 'I will make the arrangements and see to the finances, no argument.' And so Dick headed for home to tell Bertha the good news.

5. Audition time

'Good torso'

DICK'S BUSINESS CARD

Some time later in our relationship, we were standing in the wings of a theatre where Dick was about to go on as the Vicar. He was pacing up and down, checking and rechecking his props, mopping the sweat from his forehead and looking as if he might throw up at any moment. I knew better than to interrupt. Dick was enduring his nightly battle with stage fright. When the show was over and we were packing up in the dressing room he would sometimes try to explain it to me, often apologizing for being short-tempered. 'It's only nerves,' he would say, as if I didn't know.

Dick had never been able to overcome his nerves, and suffered agonies before every performance and even during filming. He blamed his emotionally disturbed childhood, which gave him a lasting inferiority complex. He talked at length about the stranglehold his mother had on him and the effect it had had on the whole of his life. He was never able to throw off his resentment of authority whether that took the form of mother, agent, employer or, later on, wife. He vividly remembered the despair he felt when, just as he was packing to go to Italy, war was declared and escape from Mother denied.

'I could taste the disappointment,' he recalled. 'But I wouldn't let all that training go to waste.' Once more Dick found himself doing the rounds of agents and producers, chasing jobs, taking anything that came along.

He had a personal card printed. *Tenor vocalist, juvenile character parts, drive any make of car. Sports: football, cricket. Knowledge of guitar. Good torso.*

Since the Chippendales weren't even a gleam in their fathers' eyes, this last humorous entry paid few, if any, dividends. Apart from his personal life, that is, which started to flourish. By now Dick Emery was seriously chasing the ladies, and his torso was put to good and frequent use.

Dick was desperate to prove his manhood. If he saw a woman he fancied he would do anything to woo her, even spending the next week's rent or borrowing money he had no hope of repaying.

His sexual appetite began to rule his life. Even though successful with women, Dick still found his nerves spoiling his work and turning auditions into nightmares.

'I'd go to an agent's office, filled with resolve, and then the old terror would return and I'd bolt like a rabbit. As for the auditions, more than once I actually had my hand raised to knock on the door – then I'd pause, think for a moment, lower my hand and slink away to the nearest café for a cup of tea, cursing myself all the while.'

He would also have to face his mother, who had always seen him out of the front door with the bright words: 'Now, dear, just think about what you're going to say when you get there.' When he kept trudging back, with another audition apparently failed, she finally lost patience and insisted on accompanying her reluctant offspring to town. That was when Dick went through the door into the inner sanctum and as often as not got the job.

Bertha's determination to see her son in the spotlight knew no bounds. On the theatrical grapevine she heard of a film producer who would be at Shepperton Studios in pre-production for a major movie.

She made Dick get into his best clobber, and went with him on the long train journey through London and out into the countryside, where they took a bus from the station to the studio entrance. There mother and son sat together on a bench by the roadside for three hours – until Bertha spotted a sleek chauffeur-driven limousine turning out of the gates and recognized her quarry in the back. She waved frantically . . . while the car drove on past with the producer studying a script and not even looking up at them.

But now came the war and the wail of sirens over London. Strangely, but with the perverseness for which the British people are famous, the theatres never had it so good. They were packed out, there were jobs going everywhere for actors and technicians, and Dick suddenly found himself in gainful employment.

By the beginning of 1940, he had still not been called up, though he had no idea why he had been overlooked. He was twenty-five, fit as a fiddle and ready to do his bit for king and country. Meantime, he won the most important role of his career; a singing part in a musical called *Land of Smiles*, and understudying the star, who happened to be the great tenor Richard Tauber. His wages were four pounds a week.

'It shows how my voice had developed that they even considered I could step into the great man's shoes in a crisis,' Dick recalled with a certain justifiable smugness. He invited Signor Cecco to the first night.

To augment his income he answered an advertisement for a chauffeur – and his business card obviously won the day, because he got the job. He reported for duty at a large house in Hampstead in the leafy heights of North London, rang the bell and found himself staring into the face of a well-known Tory MP who was also a colonel.

'He introduced me to his "dear lady wife", who was very posh, right out of the top bracket. My job was to drive her around in their huge Bentley.' The MP was stored in memory for future use as the Colonel.

'As for the lady herself, she was very grand. Her first words to me were: "Ah, Emery, the car's in the garage." I was tempted to reply: "Really, ma'am? I thought it would be in the kitchen!" But I needed the money, so I kept quiet.'

Dick recalled how the lady sat alone in the back of the massive limousine, and addressed him through the glass partition that separated them. He wore the former chauffeur's uniform – 'Unfortunately his head must have been at least two sizes larger than mine, so I would be driving her ladyship around with my head held high, and the cap stuffed with newspapers to keep it from falling over my eyes. It reminded me of the dreaded bowler when I was fifteen.'

One day the lady announced: 'Emery, I have to go to a specialist in Harley Street.' Dick recalled the scene: 'Well, that was all right – except that the poor old dear couldn't remember the number of the consulting rooms. She insisted: "I know I'll recognize it." Every few yards she would call out: "Emery, go carefully. It's the next house on the right." I'd clamp my foot on the brake, and bring the car to a shuddering halt. Stop and start, stop and start. By the time we found the right house, she was literally flat on the floor! She allowed me to drive her back to Hampstead, then fired me on the spot. "You are dismissed!" she said. I had to get the bus home. This lady was far too good a character to forget so I committed her to memory and later added a lot of her qualities to my Duchess character.'

Back in the show, Dick had no such problems and romance came on a more serious scale. The girl in question this time was a dancer in the high-kicking chorus line of *Land of Smiles*. Stage name: Zelda Barry. Her real name: Joan Sainsbury (no relation to the supermarket kings). She was a tall, slim brunette, who had a good strong singing voice and had sung with the big bands of the era, including the legendary Joe Loss Orchestra.

Dick turned on the full Emery charm and wooed her as only he could do. They soon became lovers, and set up home together in a small flat in central London. Surviving the Blitz was nothing compared to surviving his mother's criticism for his move out of her house and into the arms of 'that woman', as she put it.

But right now Dick was a lusty lad of twenty-five whose priorities were clear: making love to Zelda – and getting onstage every night, unless the wail of the air-raid sirens and the crump of exploding bombs forced them to stop until the all-clear sounded.

It was at the theatre just a few weeks later that the dreaded call-up papers finally arrived. Dick was actually standing in the wings listening to the magnificent voice of Richard Tauber when there was a hesitant tap on his arm. It was Joe, the stage doorkeeper, one of the 'good 'uns' who had become a friend to all the cast. 'Special delivery, Dick,' he whispered. 'Thought you should see it at once.' 'Thanks, Joe,' Dick whispered back, eyeing the official-looking brown envelope the way a rabbit eyes a snake. It contained his call-up papers.

Dick hadn't been looking forward to it, but he wouldn't shrink from the inevitable or shirk his duty. If he wasn't exactly action man, except between the sheets, neither was he particularly apprehensive. The War had yet to touch personally many of the young men about to face the guns across the Channel, and for Dick it was more an inconvenient interruption to his career than the prospect that he might not live to resume it.

'When do you have to leave, son?' Joe asked.

Dick looked closer. Then he blanched. 'Tonight!' he said.

That performance, Dick gave it all he'd got. And at the end, when the curtain rang down, he announced his imminent departure to the cast while they were still on stage after taking their bow. The effect was unexpected. After the initial stunned silence, the entire company gathered round to shake his hand and some even wiped a tear or two from their eyes. Dick had been an extremely popular and enthusiastic member of the cast.

Tauber himself embraced his young stand-in, then lightened the atmosphere by complaining loudly: 'They can't do this to me! What am I going to do for an understudy?'

Zelda went home with Dick, and watched in silence as he packed his things into a single case – all that was allowed the new conscripts. Like so many wartime sweethearts she felt the heart-wrenching ache of parting so soon after they had fallen in love.

His bag packed and by the front door, Dick took her hands in both of his, and looked at her with that intense stare that few women were ever able to resist. 'I don't know what's going to happen now,' he said quietly. 'Either to me or to the world. It's all going crazy. But I do know that I love you. And there's one other thing—'

'What's that?' Zelda asked, tears starting to brim in her eyes.

'Let's get married!'

How could she say no? In those few hasty seconds, with a midnight military bus waiting for him in Whitehall, they agreed to get married as soon as possible – whenever that might be.

Dick kissed his future bride a lingering farewell. 'Wish me luck,' he said, then turned and strode off into the night.

6. Duty Calls

'Pilot or nothing'

DICK, AMBITIOUS

By the time Dick told me about his adventures with the RAF we were living together in a flat in St John's Wood, London. I'll tell you how we got there later on.

He was very much affected by his surroundings and appreciated small comforts more than anyone I had met. A soft chair or a silk shirt pleased him no end, but his favourite 'bit of pampering', as he called it, was to be brought a cup of tea in bed with plenty of time to wake up slowly and quietly. When I asked him why this was so very important, he said it began as far back as his first days in the RAF, where he was jolted into the early morning by a bugle and surrounded by the din of men swearing and stomping about, lighting up cigarettes and yelling at each other. The uniform didn't fit and was scratchy and there was no tea for hours.

In the theatre it was late to bed, late to rise and no matter what the circumstances, very few performers sparkle early in the morning and definitely not before tea.

Propped up by a bank of pillows, clutching the essential mug of tea, Dick remembered his first rude awakening in the RAF.

'After I had said goodbye to Zelda, I just managed to catch the midnight bus to Northolt and found myself sharing a dormitory with a bunch of strangers. We all felt a mixture of excitement, resentment and apprehension at what lay ahead. The RAF was a pretty obvious choice for me as I was obsessed with speed and already fascinated by planes. The prospect of actually flying one attracted me like a magnet. But I was in trouble right from the first day, when the senior officer asked me what I wanted to be.

'"Pilot or nothing," I replied with conviction.

'"Can you tell me how many degrees you would pass through if you made a right-angle turn?"

'Mathematics not being one of my best subjects, I couldn't answer immediately and before I could work it out he barked: "Right, Emery. You'll be better suited as an aircraftman than a pilot. Training is in Scotland."'

And so Aircraftman Emery duly reported for twelve weeks training, which he hated, longing to be reunited with Zelda and theatrical friends. He even missed his mother!

'It made me change my mind about the RAF, and I was arrogant enough to think I could get away with bucking the system. I tried to do it my way – not cleaning my boots, leaving my bed unmade, late for duty. You name it, I did it. The result was that I was always on a charge, and got a reputation as a troublemaker.'

After twelve weeks getting to know what makes a plane tick, the reluctant rookie was posted to RAF Halton in Buckinghamshire with the rank of Aircraftman Second Class, lowest of the low. The training for which Dick was so supremely ungrateful – paid for courtesy of His Majesty's Government – would in fact be a vital asset to him when he took up serious flying as a hobby, and started buying his own planes. But for now, it was simply a pain.

Maintaining the planes that took off day and night on bombing missions, many never to return, left Dick with one bizarre image he could never erase from his mind: the station's padre, walking between the great Lancasters bristling with bombs and with gun turrets fore and aft – 'and sprinkling holy water and blessing their missions of death and destruction.'

Dick had no formal religious upbringing, but what he saw disturbed him greatly, and he put it in simple terms: 'What I'd learned of a supposedly loving God I just could not equate with what I saw happening all around me.'

His nearest brush with an early death came when he was on 'weapon guard duty' one evening. Crouched behind sandbags in a dugout at one end of the runway behind an ancient 40-pounder, Dick and a fellow rookie named Bobby, who had become a good pal, were keeping their spirits up in time-honoured fashion by singing songs from the old musicals.

'*When the red, red robin . . .*'

Suddenly a roar filled the sky, drowning their voices. Dick had a brief, unnerving glimpse of an enormous shadow passing directly overhead, before the sound of gunfire chattered above them, and bullets sprayed across the tarmac and burst their sandbags wide open. It was a German plane, very low, and by the time Dick had struggled to the controls and fired a few useless salvos into the sky, the intruder was gone.

Dick started up the song again – to find himself singing alone. 'I looked around for my buddy – and he was lying there practically cut in two. I called for the padre on the field telephone – before I threw up.'

There was help at hand in the shape of Sergeant Frank Gray, who had been in charge of Dick and the new arrivals from Scotland. Despite his authority and a voice that could stop a tank at a hundred yards, Sergeant Gray was a kindly soul, and he saw hidden depths in the raw new rebel under his command.

The sergeant, who for some reason was known to one and all as 'Charlie', took Dick into an empty office, sat the young recruit down, and had a heart-to-heart chat with him. 'He didn't tear me off a strip, as he could have done,' Dick recalled. 'Instead he asked me about my background and my career, what I enjoyed doing most, and how I could make the best of it in the RAF. The thing is, I was never noisy or rude. I was just quietly rebellious – and Charlie saw through it.'

The result was that Dick started helping out with the camp entertainment – camp as in tent. He was promoted to Aircraftman First Class. With his new-found enthusiasm and talent, he soon led the troupe with his singing, tap-dancing and comedy sketches.

Sergeant Gray would say later: 'Dick was basically shy, keeping himself very much to himself. But once he got up onto a stage, we saw the other side of him – a terrific personality, a wonderful tenor voice and a tremendous sense of humour.'

Dick in turn repaid the compliment. 'Thanks to that man, I stopped being just a number and found some self-respect. I smartened myself up, and started taking a genuine interest in life on the base.' After the war, 'Charlie' Gray became a friend for life.

But the mutual admiration society did become slightly strained when Charlie, Dick and six of his fellow recruits were on guard duty one bitter winter's night. Two hours on, two hours off, in shifts. The only good news about guard duty was that they were given special privileges in the form of steak for breakfast at the end of their stint.

One man would be detailed to cook all eight steaks, and have them ready when the others came bursting into the cookhouse, freezing – but happily off duty, and hardly able to wait for their culinary reward. Only this time an empty table and a guilt-ridden Leading Aircraftman (Dick had gone up another notch) mumbled excuses and was looking for the nearest exit. 'Fellers, I just don't know where they are . . .' But someone did.

Sergeant Gray led the investigation, and finally came up with the answer. Dick had spent his 'cooking' hours in the warmth of the boiler room because it was so cold outside – and given all the steaks to the boilermen as the sweetener to let him in! 'I could have done with one of those steaks for the black eye I got,' Dick said ruefully.

But this was a small hiccup in what looked like a promising career in those early days of the War. Dick was promoted to Corporal and Zelda was able to join him on the base for some of the concerts, taking part in the entertainment that helped keep the morale high among the 'desperately young' airmen who knew that tomorrow's sortie might be their last.

Then came a new posting – to RAF Station St Eval, in Cornwall. There, in nearby Bodmin on 6 November 1940, Dick and Zelda were married, though after a brief honeymoon the bride had to move back to London as there were no married quarters for a corporal in St Eval.

For eighteen months life was tolerable. Zelda came to visit as often as she could, sometimes to take part in a concert and sometimes just for a cuddle, and on 11 July 1942 she gave birth to their son, Gilbert Richard Emery. Dick was overjoyed and determined to be the best possible father. But almost at once everything started to go wrong.

Married pay for a corporal wasn't very much, and Zelda couldn't work because of the baby – added to which Dick also had to keep his mother. When he got leave Dick would hitch-hike up to London to find his wife depressed and resentful, with a baby to look after and no more glamorous work. He rolled his sleeves up and literally scrubbed the flat right through, doing all the jobs that Zelda 'just hadn't got round to'. Having sorted them out he had to go and do the same for his mother, who was feeling very neglected. She hated sharing her son with a wife and didn't care for being a 'granny' at all.

Instead of uniting and helping each other and thereby Dick, the two women in his life quite literally pulled him apart. Trying to keep them both going financially and physically, mostly by remote control, finally proved too much. It wasn't as if he felt essential to the RAF – most of the time he spent peeling potatoes for fifteen hundred men. Anyone could do that, he thought, but no one else could look after his wife, son and mother. He had to get out of the RAF and back to the theatre, where he could earn enough money to keep everyone going.

This seemed clear and sensible to Dick. He didn't feel like a vital cog in the war effort or see the big picture of self-sacrifice by so many. All he saw was his family needing him and he answered their need in the only way he thought he could. By becoming a deserter.

When he was telling this, I noticed that Dick's fingers had gone white as he gripped the empty mug. He looked sad and appalled at what he had done so many years before. He kept telling me how ashamed he felt on looking back, but at the time he was convinced it was the only thing he could do.

'Would you like another tea?' was all I could say.

'Oh yes please,' he said gratefully. He cupped his hands round the hot mug as if he was freezing and went back to the story.

'That evening I packed a bag and walked calmly through the gates of the camp, flashing my evening pass at the guard. I was out and not coming back.

'I thought I should put as much distance between myself and the base, so Scotland seemed the logical answer. Zelda met me at Paddington and we talked through the plans. At last she agreed it was the only thing to do.

'"Keep in touch," she begged.

'"Open a PO box in your maiden name of Sainsbury and I'll send money as often as I can, I promise." She trusted me.

'"I'll call you, don't worry and I'll deal with Mother later."'

That was all the time there was before heading for Euston and the train to Glasgow.

Once there he melted into the anonymous side streets around the station, booking into a succession of boarding houses. In those days, with other young men going AWOL rather than do their bit for the war effort, he thought it was unlikely that his photograph would ever appear in a rogues' gallery or on a poster outside a local police station. But the Military Police were less casual and certainly less forgiving. The hunt was soon on for Corporal Emery, and he knew they would never rest until he was back in the ranks – with a spell behind bars as a warm-up.

Dick dealt with his mother by saying he was on a 'secret mission' and couldn't divulge his whereabouts. This was theatrical enough for her to believe him.

He spent the next six months in a state of high stress, moving around various cheap bed and breakfast lodgings where they took ready cash and didn't ask questions. He never stayed longer than a week and remained in his room all day, emerging at night to earn 'a few quid' in a bar or a café, and even from the odd theatrical date. He changed his name almost as often as his job, signing himself Dick Smart or Richard Gilbert and a variety of other names that he hoped wouldn't raise an eyebrow or a suspicion.

'I was in a constant sweat, a continual state of panic,' he admitted. 'Every shadow made me jump. I couldn't help feeling that people were looking at me, and if I saw a uniform I would just slink into the nearest doorway and try to look as if I was on an errand, or doing *something*.'

Somehow he got away with it. Glasgow had more to worry about than an extra vagrant on the streets, with the bombing of the docks and general concern over the War. Dick sent brown envelopes back to London, and Zelda duly collected them. After a few weeks the heat seemed to be off.

Now the fugitive took a chance. He heard they were casting for a big West End musical in London: *The Merry Widow,* which would run for more than a year at Her Majesty's Theatre. Dick took the train south, and headed for the Stage Door. Somehow he managed to infiltrate the chorus line; there were still enough young men around who for health and other reasons could make up a chorus. He sank into deliberate obscurity as just another of the agile performers who were all dressed alike – complete with large ear-to-ear moustaches that covered most of their faces.

The stars in Franz Lehar's sparkling light operetta were Cyril Richard and Madge Elliot, and Dick pranced around on the stage with the best of them, feeling safe for the first time since he'd gone AWOL.

He moved back with Zelda and for seven weeks they enjoyed a semblance of family life, with the curtain going up in the evenings without incident. Even the money was better. The bills were paid and Dick started to relax.

Then one night two sergeants from Dick's squadron came to see the show. Even from the back of the stalls they recognized the familiar figure from the camp entertainment.

Next night, the visitors that Dick had been dreading arrived at the Stage Door. Two Redcaps marched in, informed the startled doorman who they were, showed him a photo of the wanted man, and strode off into the wings. The Merry Widow Waltz was in full swing, and as Dick pirouetted off in his ruffled shirt, velvet jacket and satin breeches, two pairs of strong arms reached out and grabbed him, before hauling him off to his dressing room.

There was no time to change. 'Get your things in a bag, sonny, and come with us!' ordered the first Redcap. 'Don't even worry about the whiskers.'

The cast was still giving full vent to the Merry Widow Waltz as Dick was marched out into the street in his costume and bundled into a waiting van. Despite his protestations the burly escorts had no time for mercy.

That night the chorus was one short, though it is doubtful if anyone outside the cast noticed.

7. In the Slammer

'Scrub it with a toothbrush'

PRISON GUARD

It took a great many more mugs of tea before Dick could bear to relive the horror and shame of prison life. But he wanted me to know *everything*.

MPs (the military sort, that is) don't mess about. Their bewhiskered prisoner was driven twenty miles north of London and straight to Stanmore Military Prison, which had a reputation among raw recruits akin to Alcatraz at its worst. At least they allowed him to change out of his satin breeches and into his civvy garb in the van. Dick would remain incarcerated in the slammer for nine 'ghastly' months, during which time he was put through the kind of degradation that would have broken another man's spirit.

For starters, once the 'tache was removed – his stripes went with it. Corporal Emery became just another bad boy on the block. His cell was a soulless cage measuring twelve feet by eight; he shared it with another 'runner', and would for ever after remember the lack of privacy, even to fulfil the basic human needs.

But beyond the physical wretchedness – no soap, foul food and lack of creature comforts – lay a deeper problem, a sense of guilt and shame that gnawed at Dick like a cancer.

No one wanted to know why he had deserted. No one cared. Dick had expected to be interrogated at the very least – but no top brass turned up to question him. He had brought dishonour to himself, and to the comrades who had taken him on trust to fight the common foe – that was the message, loud and clear. Perhaps if someone had given him a chance, Dick would have explained. He found himself being given 'the treatment' instead – a particularly humiliating retribution reserved for any of the inmates who got on the wrong side of the guards. Dick managed to do this the moment he heard the gates clang behind him.

One of the guards, a tough sergeant who might have been a model for the ferocious 'Fatso' Judson in *From Here to Eternity,* took a particular dislike to the new arrival. A huge man with bulging eyes and a Hitler moustache, he was known (behind his back) as Adolph. You crossed him at your peril, and when Dick did so – he could never remember exactly how – he was given 'latrine duty'.

Cleaning out the toilets at the end of the block meant going down on his hands and knees to scrub away for half an hour every day until the tiles shone. One day he got a sense of things to come when Sergeant Adolph strode in with a bucket of foul slops from the nearest cell, emptied it over the tiles, then ordered: 'Do it again!' The following week the sergeant imposed a new diversion: 'Scrub each lavatory seat with your toothbrush, sonny boy!' he barked. 'That should improve your smile!'

This was too much for Dick to take. But Adolph stood six foot four and Dick was five six, and anyway he didn't dare even to think of the punishment that he'd get if he stepped out of line. But there were other ways to exact revenge. Dick had a word with the prison cook. The result was a large slice of ginger cake which he managed to smuggle into his cell. When latrine duty came around, he took the cake with him. Left alone in the first cubicle he cleaned the seat as never before and then arranged the cake all round it. He was several cubicles on, cleaning away innocently enough, when half an hour later Adolph arrived to inspect the work. He eyed the first seat in disbelief. 'Look at this!' he roared. 'It's filthy! Clean it up!' A penitent Dick looked at the seat. 'I can do better than that, sarge,' he said humbly – and knelt down and proceeded to stuff the brown mess into his mouth. 'Christ!' exclaimed Sergeant Adolph, turning green. He stumbled into the next cubicle, and Dick heard satisfying retching noises from the basin. He was taken off latrine duty that day, and never had to do it again.

Apart from a few humorous interludes, this was a terrible time for Dick. The realization of what he had done weighed him down, added to which he was now unable to support his wife, son and mother even as well as he had before as most of his pay was stopped while he was in prison.

His mother came to visit and made it very clear how disappointed she was in him, especially for breaking his promise to support her. She had to go back to work for a few months, which didn't please her at all.

Zelda also had to work. But for her, getting a babysitter and returning to her glamorous life was not such a hardship. She went to see Dick occasionally, taking baby Gill with her, but the visits were infrequent and strained. Dick had to watch his marriage falling apart and there was nothing he could do but blame himself. He missed his baby son terribly and wrote to Zelda, begging her to wait for him and to bring the baby to see him more often.

But eventually it became obvious that the marriage was not going to survive. Their relationship was getting worse, with every visit spent in argument. Zelda wanted a divorce and Dick, although very sad, couldn't blame her. Finally he signed the necessary papers, not knowing that she had already met a GI and was planning to go to America, taking baby Gill with her. Dick was heartbroken at parting with his son, even more so because he eventually lost touch with Zelda, who married her GI in 1946. Dick didn't see Gill again until thirty-three years later.

Dick was released from Stanmore Military Prison in 1943, having survived on his wits and humour. He couldn't wait to get through the gates, but once outside he paused to give a mock salute to Adolph whom he spotted behind the wire fence. He received a last scowl to send him on his way.

8. The Gang's All Here!

'Didn't you hear the bugle?'

DICK TO THE GANG

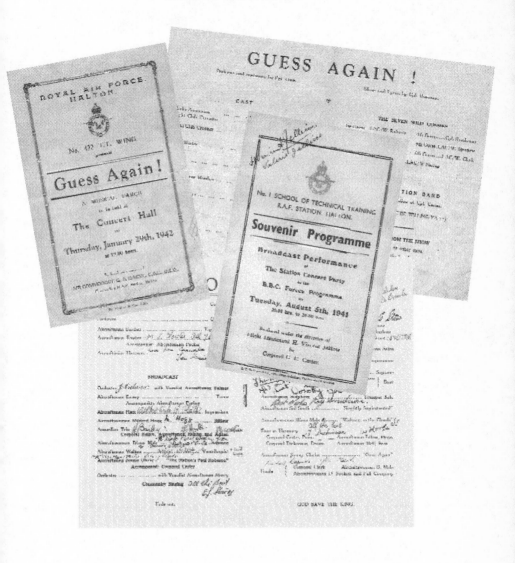

It might appear that Dick was deliberately rebellious, precious about himself or even cowardly. But from what I learnt about his character, his ability to identify with others, and the acute awareness and susceptibility to his surroundings which enabled him to do such brilliant characterizations, could not be turned on and off at will. Add to that his lack of confidence masked by theatrical behaviour, and there was a disaster waiting to happen when he was confined to a conventional rough-and-ready male world such as the RAF.

The Gang Show was what saved him and gave him the opportunity to retain his sensitivity, romantic nature and humour whilst enabling him to do his bit for the war effort. He was much happier when talking about his Gang Show days, and never more so than on one wet afternoon in Hull. We were there for a week while Dick was performing in his theatre show.

It was the 1st of March, which happened to be my birthday, but Dick hadn't mentioned it that morning so I thought he'd forgotten. We had to go out on business, followed by an uneventful lunch and back to the hotel in the pouring rain. I was trying not to feel depressed as Dick opened the door to our suite and stood back in his gentlemanly way to let me go in first. One step inside the room, I stopped in amazement. The whole place was full of pink roses. Tables, chairs, the bed, window sills and book shelves were stacked with vases or piles of roses and the floor was strewn with petals. The bathroom was the same. The bath was full of long-stemmed buds and even the loo had been used as a vase! I was speechless with delight as Dick waltzed me around on the carpet of petals, singing 'Happy Birthday To You', over and over again. There was a knock on the door and a waiter appeared with a trolley full of tea and a large pink birthday cake complete with candles. We cleared a couple of chairs and tucked into the feast. I was so glad that Dick hadn't had the romance knocked out of him.

As we munched our pink cake we chatted as usual and soon Dick was reminiscing again. This time it was about the Gang Show and how thankful he was to have been part of it. Once again I sat enthralled while he chatted on, stopping only to open the window as we were nearly asphyxiated by the overpowering smell of roses! That day in 1943 fresh air and freedom had never tasted so good. Except that Dick wasn't exactly free, he still had to do his bit for the war effort – and this time, no messing about like going on the run again! He had learnt his lesson, paid his dues, grown to love ginger cake, and now it was payback time. Dick felt he owed his country something – only what?

'I want to be a despatch rider,' he announced to the senior officer, a colonel, who interviewed him following his discharge from prison. 'I know about bikes, and I like to ride fast. I'll be an asset to the side!' Maybe it was the oxygen of freedom, but Dick was feeling cocky that day.

'Umm,' said the colonel, shuffling through his papers. 'I presume you mean our side?' Ex-Corporal Emery's record was not exactly one to inspire confidence in the ranks.

In the stuffy office at RAF Hendon, an aide stood by the desk. He cleared his throat. 'Excuse me, sir.' Then he looked at Dick. 'Weren't you in show business?' Dick nodded and reeled off a list of musicals and plays on his CV. The aide said to the colonel: 'How about the RAF Gang Show, sir? They're looking for people.' The colonel sat back, eyeing Dick closely for a long minute. Then he nodded, and picked up a pen. 'Good idea. We'll arrange an audition for you.'

Two days later in London, clutching a dog-eared song sheet and with more nerves than ever before, Dick reported to Howton House, Kingsway, for an audition in front of the legendary Ralph Reader. He caught a glimpse of the forty-year-old producer, a burly, authoritative figure in a loud sports jacket and thick-rimmed glasses, before being hustled away to wait his turn. The auditions were being conducted in a

large rehearsal room, with a few chairs drawn up in the middle and a lot
of space at the front as the 'stage'.

The roots of the Gang Show go back to October 1932, when the
breezy, never-take-no-for-an-answer young impresario Reader wrote
and produced a three-night review for the Scala Theatre in the West
End of London. Ten years later, in the wartime setting, it spawned
talents like Peter Sellers, Harry Worth, Tony Hancock and many more.
Ralph had appeared in the original himself, singing 'The Best Things in
Life Are Free', which later became one of the show's great numbers.

Ralph was born in Somerset and brought up by various aunts and
uncles after both his parents died. When he was eighteen he headed for
America and made his mark on Broadway, where he became known as
the 'The Kid Dance Director'. He went onto work all over the USA and
nearer home in Europe.

Losing his parents at an early age, fending for himself and travelling
the world gave Ralph a better-than-normal awareness of people and he
was able to spot 'talent' at once. Dick didn't know all this as he sat
shivering with nerves, waiting his turn to audition. He heard the call
'Next' – and he was 'on'.

He took a deep breath, held his song sheet in both hands to stop it
shaking and marched into the empty space, radiating confidence. Before
he could do more than reach the centre and open his mouth, a voice
boomed out: 'Okay. You'll do!' Dick stood very still for a long moment,
then hurried off before Mr Reader could change his mind. Long
afterwards, when he was a stalwart in the troupe, he asked the veteran
producer why he had been picked like that, unheard and virtually
unseen. 'It was the way you walked out. Very professional. Good presence,' the big man told him.

The years of his mother's coaching had paid off. Dick had been
spotted in less than two seconds by the showman who for the next three
years would become his mentor and friend, revealing for Dick his true
calling and restoring his confidence.

'Show business is a profession in which we are all part of a brother-
hood,' Reader lectured Dick like the father he never really knew.

'There's a bond between us that is found in no other calling. You can
leave it, but you will never forget it, and for the rest of your life you will

long for it. It's the most contradictory profession in the world – the longer you are in it, the less you know! There are never any certainties, it's all guesswork. But you'll have fun – and meet some tremendous characters.'

Ralph loved to talk about how the RAF Gang Show started. The top brass had decided that entertainment was going to play a vital role in the war effort. He was called into Head Office and told: 'If you can find enough men who can be moulded into a show, we'll let you have them. You can call your unit "Ralph Reader and Ten Blokes from the Gang Show"!'

They started out on the coat-tails of ENSA – Entertainments National Service Association – the original forces show that Tommy Trinder dubbed 'Every Night Something Awful!' There was nothing awful about it for Dick. He was in heaven, blissfully unaware of the more serious side to the Gang Show tours, which were used by RAF Intelligence as a cover for 'special jobs' to do with propaganda and liaising with local overseas agents.

Dick was sent to Number One Unit, RAF Lincoln, which must have been one of the smallest units in the RAF, being comprised of only ten men, plus Ralph Reader himself who took part in the shows 'out front' whenever he could. The lads called him 'Chief' because 'Ralph' was too intimate and 'sir' just didn't sound right.

In all, there would be twenty-four Gang Show units working in bases throughout Britain, and further afield when the call came.

On his first morning, the sound of the 6.00 a.m. bugle and Reveille had Dick leaping out of bed and heading for the washroom. Force of habit by now. After a shower and a shave he hurried back to begin struggling into his uniform, when he noticed something. The hut was uncommonly quiet. No one else had moved. Nine other figures in the neighbouring beds slumbered blissfully on. The only sound was the occasional snore. 'Christ!' said Dick aloud. He shook the lump in the next bed. 'Quick, get up! You'll be late for inspection. Didn't you hear the bugle?'

A sleepy eye squinted up at him from the pillow: 'Go back to bed. We never get up till 9.30!' That was the first hint for Dick, clambering gratefully back into bed, that he might have stumbled into something rather special. The second was when the Quartermaster handed him a pair of pyjamas – blue silk pyjamas with his personal initials mono-grammed on the pocket!

Now Dick started noticing other things. The other nine lads had longer hair, neatly cut and not cropped by a hasty pair of scissors in the barber's shop on the base. Their uniforms were tailored to fit, and always looked crisp and fresh. The onerous duties he had endured before, like peeling potatoes for fifteen hundred men as he had done in Cornwall, were non-existent, light at the very worst. 'All our time and energy went into preparing and rehearsing the shows,' he said, recalling those first halcyon days when the earlier, unfortunate months now receded into nothing more than a bad dream.

Stories filtered back about the adventures of his fellow artistes, and the mishaps that went hand in glove with the job. Cardew 'the Cad' Robinson was performing in an outdoor theatre when a rocket was accidentally released from a stationary plane on the tarmac nearby. It went hurtling through the backcloth behind him, exploding on the edge of the airfield. Cardew's response when he had regained his feet was typically him! He turned to a group of airmen sitting on the grass and enquired: 'Whose side are you on? We can't be *that* bad!'

Another time, Dick chortled, Reader and his merry men flew into a remote base in Africa to find the audience of airmen chanting: 'Bring 'em out! Where are they?' They discovered that instead of the official billing *Ralph Reader and Ten Blokes from the Gang Show,* some joker had pinned up: *Ralph Reader and Ten Blondes . . .*

Ralph was particularly fond of telling another story of a young airman he auditioned, who told him he played the drums. 'Anything else?' the Chief enquired.

'Well, I can do a few impressions.'

Reader ordered the potential recruit to report next day in the NAAFI at 10.00 a.m. At the appointed hour the Chief strolled in through the rear door – to hear his own voice coming from the bar singing 'We're Riding Along on the Crest of a Wave'. Putting his head round the door, Ralph saw the young airman giving a truly incredible impersonation of him. The other airmen in the bar abruptly stopped laughing. The comic turned, saw the Chief in the doorway, and snapped into a salute. He then enquired with amazing panache: 'Sir, am I on a charge – or are you thirsty?' Ralph decided he was thirsty, had a beer with the cheeky newcomer – and Peter Sellers became part of the Gang on the spot.

Within weeks, Dick was on the road. First stop, Italy. Each member of the Gang was provided with his personal 'skip', a large square basket in which he kept all his costumes, props and make-up. They travelled in a three-ton lorry that became their mobile home. Dick recalled being squashed in the back in semi-darkness for hours at a time – but he was in his element.

'We'd sing and tell stupid jokes, each of us trying to outdo the next man. When we finally reached our destination, there would be a mad rush to find a corner to change in, usually as close to the stage as possible.'

'We could be out in the open in a field with a makeshift stage they'd cobbled together from nowhere. Or indoors in a NAAFI hut, which would be an overheated smoke-filled bar. It didn't matter. We were there to make them laugh and forget the fighting for a few precious hours, and we became one big family show. There was nothing like it, before or since.

'Some of the lads would be going out next day, and might never return. We knew it, they knew it – but our job was to make sure they didn't think about it.'

After Italy, the unit went to East Africa, Egypt, Palestine, the Persian Gulf, Iceland and anywhere else it was needed.

In early 1944 a newspaper reported:

The Gang Show played on board the ships escorting the surrendering Italian fleet. They travelled in lorries between Tripoli and Tunis and took eight weeks to complete the journey, living entirely on corned beef and biscuits, and were once lost in the desert. The average working day of a Gang Show airman is 16 hours. Work out for yourself what it must be like, where amenities can often be counted on the fingers of a bloke giving the V-sign! They're a great bunch . . .

Dick was there.

In all, according to War Office statistics, more than three and a half million servicemen were entertained during the War, with the Gang Show travelling three hundred and forty thousand miles to take their bow.

9. Front Line

'Better in drag than combat gear'

DICK

Dick and I did a huge amount of driving during our time together. Around the UK from theatre to theatre, and hundreds of miles more in New Zealand and Australia. We took it in turns to drive, two hours on and two off. Whoever was 'off' had to talk non-stop to keep the other awake. Dick needed very little prompting to talk about his Gang Show days. He had wonderful, happy memories of what must, in reality, have been uncomfortable and dangerous times. But all he remembered was the companionship, humour and at last doing something he was good at.

Dick was now one of the Gang, a leading light who was popular with his nine comrades for his ready wit and generous nature. When they reached Naples, he could count as many as fourteen costume changes in a show – 'Speed was all important' – as they dived around backstage trying not to bump into the scenery or into each other.

But once, looking for an easier way to get through the show, he made a big mistake. The curtain was due up in ten minutes. Everyone was piling off the communal lorry to grab their spot to change. Dick was last off.

'Amid the usual chaos, it suddenly occurred to me: wait a minute! Why go in there with the crowd? The lorry was backed up close to the door of the hut where we were going to perform, so why not use it as my private dressing room?

'I spread my costumes out, all fourteen of them, and sat down in front of a makeshift mirror to put on my make-up. That's when the lorry started to move!

'I shouted fit to bust, yelling out of the back to attract the driver's attention – no joy. I couldn't get through to the front because it was blocked. I was stuck.

'The lorry went on for three miles and ended up in the middle of a field. Don't ask me why. All I know is that it took all my pleading and cajoling to get the driver to take me back, and I missed the first half of the show. After that I stuck with the boys.'

Whether that episode ever got to the ears of Ralph Reader was never known. But a week later Dick found himself, along with two of his mates, promoted to Corporal. 'I suppose you could say I was reinstated, but I just couldn't believe my luck; I knew we might all be killed at any time, because we really were in the front line, so we just took every day as it came. The only thing that mattered was the show.

'We were never armed. All we had to defend ourselves with was a stick of greasepaint to hurl at the enemy!'

Without warning Dick and his unit were flown back to England. They were given seven days' leave before 'a big job', which turned out to be the invasion of Normandy. The Gang were sworn to secrecy, forbidden to talk to anyone – not even their nearest and dearest – about where they might be heading or what might be in the wind. Not that they had any idea – but rumours abounded.

Back home, Bertha was up to her usual tricks. Knowing her beloved boy was back, she plagued Headquarters with phone calls demanding to speak to 'Dickie'. Apparently, no one had ever heard of him and the switchboard was not amused. Then she found out that the unit was due back at Howton House, and was waiting by the entrance when the Gang's lorry pulled up.

Dick spotted her before she spotted him, leaped over the tailboard and hared away up the street to hide in doorways until she gave up. She asked the rest of the troupe where her Dickie was. When they all professed ignorance, the sight of her dejected face moved them so much that they took pity on her. 'Come back this evening, luv, and we'll get you into the camp,' one of the corporals said quietly.

He passed the word around to the others, and when the lorry took off in the direction of RAF Station, Harrow, Bertha was aboard. At the base, they smuggled her through the gates under a blanket, and gave her a slap-up meal in the mess, even though her errant son was conspicuous by his absence. They got her out again, with a firm promise that Dick would phone her the very next day. Which is exactly what he did when he heard how his mates had treated his dear, if tiresome, mum.

18 June 1944. D-Day plus thirteen. Number One Unit was piled into a Dakota heading out of Southampton, bound for Normandy, flying low over the Channel.

Sitting with his back against the hard steel of the plane's interior, Dick looked at his comrades and suddenly realized again how defenceless they all were. No one had issued them with parachutes, let alone weapons, and here they were heading unescorted into the hostile fields of France.

To keep up their spirits, the unit sang – and many of them said an inward prayer. Ralph Reader was leading them from the front, as always. After a word with the pilot he returned to the main cabin. 'Listen, lads, I've got news for you. There's no airfield!' The team gawped at each other blankly. 'Where are we going to land, Chief? On the beach?' 'Don't worry, he'll find us somewhere . . .' At which point the captain's voice came tinnily through the tannoy: 'Ten seconds, everyone. Hang on and hold tight!' The Dakota crash-landed among the dunes but by some miracle no one was hurt.

They piled out in a threshing scrum, dragging their skips behind them, racing for the nearest cover as the sound of gunfire and whining shells filled the air around them. Finally they met up in a nearby apple orchard and huddled in an untidy group wondering what to do and where to go. Reader had disappeared to find the top brass and discuss the tour ahead, and they suddenly felt very alone. Apart from writing the scripts and directing the shows, the Chief was in charge of all the hour-to-hour arrangements of the team of stalwarts, and took pride in the job.

But now the sound of heavy artillery and the rattle of gunfire seemed so dangerously close it might have come from the next field. Every few seconds the ground shook under their feet. Crouched beside an apple tree, Dick looked apprehensively through the branches in case a German helmet popped up with a gun pointed in their direction. It crossed his mind that his unit was more used to appearing in funny costumes and even in drag than in combat gear in the middle of a fire-fight.

'Oi, you lot!' A figure appeared from nowhere, not a German but a British sergeant with a loud voice and an armful of shovels. He dumped them unceremoniously on the ground, and ordered: 'Get digging!'

'What do you mean, Sarge?' one of the braver members of the troupe ventured. 'Dig what?'

'What I mean is that if you want to live till morning, start digging! You're spending the night here.' The sergeant's glare was enough to catapult the Gang into action.

Dick recalled: 'The gunfire had eased off. We each dug a hole deep enough to take us and our skip. We found branches, pieces of metal, anything to make the hides. Then, as darkness fell, the bombardment started again. Shells were detonating everywhere, and shrapnel was whistling past us. It seemed to come from every direction, and everywhere you looked the sky was lit up.

'Number One Unit disappeared into our holes like rabbits, and we lay quaking as the world seemed to explode around us. But somehow I felt safe enough down there, and even if we didn't get any sleep we all survived the night.'

Two days later it was safe to move on. The Chief appeared, armed with a map, and went over the plans like a military operation – which, after all, it was!

Dick's closest pals were Fred and Frank Cox, the 'terrible twins', he called them, always ready with a gag to keep the team's spirits up. On the second night, with the gunfire temporarily stilled, Dick was sleeping fitfully in his foxhole when there was a tap on the sheet of corrugated iron he had employed as a makeshift roof.

He froze as he heard a German voice say: 'You in sere, mein Herr. Come out mit your hands raised!'

Quivering, Dick slid back the sheet, to peer up into the laughing faces of Frank and Fred. 'Gotcha, Dick!'

'Why, you! I could have shot you.'

'You're forgetting something. We don't have any guns!'

'Well – I can do a lot with a stick of greasepaint,' Dick warned darkly.

The tour took them to Bayon, Carne, Ypres, on up to Antwerp and all over Holland as the German war machine pulled back and freedom started to appear a reality. In all, the Gang were on the road for three months, staging their shows in barns, town halls, Nissen huts and open fields while the summer held.

As a last resort, they'd turn the rear of the lorry into a stage and put the show on there.

They never knew how many people would be out there waiting for song, dance and laughter to lift their spirits – hundreds usually or sometimes just a handful. 'No matter how few, we always gave them the complete show,' Dick said. By now he was experimenting with a diverse cast of characters, all of them his own inventions. Ralph Reader wrote the sketches, but allowed – in fact, encouraged – the lads to put in their own material, and as often as not much of it was improvised on the night. There were no girls in the show, which meant a spot of drag 'for glamour'. Vera Lynn, of course, was the Forces' Sweetheart. Dick, greatly daring, created a character called Vera Thin, who was a big hit.

You could hardly call their tour of duty five-star luxury. Conditions generally, Dick recalled, were 'terrible'. Apart from the emotional trauma of seeing the dead and wounded brought back from the front lines, there was the constant tension of attack from the air or a surprise bombardment from out of nowhere – which often happened. Their lorry became a cocoon for the 'family' and if they couldn't sleep aboard they would kip out underneath it on field stretchers they had acquired as makeshift beds.

We were in our final home in Shepperton when Dick told me this next part of the story. There was bright sunlight shining through the leaves of an apple tree, making a mottled pattern on our sitting-room carpet. I looked up to see Dick leaping from one shadow to the next, hiding behind chairs as he went. Even for Dick, this was unusual behaviour so I asked him what he was up to. All the time he told me this story he continued to hop round the sitting room, eventually dis-appearing behind the sofa only to re-emerge a few seconds later brandishing an imaginary rifle!

During the hectic months in Europe Dick became known as the 'magpie' – meaning that he would wander off on his own looking for souvenirs to take home. His personal skip grew heavier by the week, with all sorts of trinkets and even sharp pieces of shrapnel that he just couldn't resist.

He was almost (but not quite) cured of this habit on a day in northern France when he spotted an abandoned German rifle lying in the middle of a field. The group was on foot, heading for its next date with the troops. Without thinking, Dick dashed away from the marching line, and ran into the field. He had reached the gun, and was just picking it up when there was a bellow from the edge of the field.

'Dick – stay right where you are! Don't *move*!' It was the Cox twins who realized Dick had unknowingly walked across a minefield.

It took Dick the longest hour of his life to retrace his path, stubbornly clutching the gun and stepping gingerly into his own footprints in the mud while his mates ducked down in a ditch – just in case.

On this occasion the Cox twins probably saved his life, and at least he managed to keep his trophy.

When this tour for the Number One Unit came to an end, they were transferred back to home ground, but were soon off again to entertain the men in the isolated coastal command posts.

First stop was the Outer Hebrides and another hilarious happening. Dick and a chap called John had to wear crinolines for the grand finale. The only way they could get into these huge hooped dresses was to climb onto a chair and actually jump into them. There was very little space behind the makeshift backcloth and not much time. It was panic stations, especially when John lost his balance and missed the voluminous dress. He crashed to the floor, dragging the backcloth with him. Dick was left standing on his chair in full view of the entire audience, with only a minuscule jockstrap for cover! Like the true professional that he was, Dick milked the situation as if it had been heaven-sent, and almost convinced his audience that it was all part of the act.

Next stop was the Orkneys, those windswept and storm-tossed islands at the very north of Scotland where, as Dick said, 'you wear a kilt at your peril'. The local padre would go by rowing boat from one island to another to take Holy Communion, and after meeting the Gang he invited two of them to accompany him on his weekly mission.

Dick was one of the volunteers and off they went in a small rowing boat, with Dick in charge of the bread and wine. On the first leg, the weather grew stormier by the minute, the sea rougher and the stomachs of the pair of landlubbers more delicate.

'Try a little sip of wine, boys,' the kindly padre suggested. 'It'll help settle you.' Dick remembered: 'It was a long slow journey. By the time we reached the first island we were both happily drunk and there was no wine left for the Communion services. For some reason, we weren't asked again . . .'

One of the privileges for the Gang Show was the prized late pass, which entitled them to stay out of camp until midnight. Whenever possible, all ten of them (the Chief being somewhere overseas) surged off happily to the nearest pub, where they celebrated in style. Drink followed drink, and on this particular night the local malt whisky proved too attractive to ignore. Suddenly it was one o'clock in the morning and they were out of time and out of bounds.

'We staggered back to the camp, but even in our condition we realized the main gate would not be a good idea,' Dick recalled. 'The camp was protected by huge coils of barbed wire and a high fence, with guards patrolling at regular intervals.

'Fuelled with Dutch courage, we decided to try the fence. Keeping as quiet as we could, we managed to pull three of the planks away and crawled through – until one of us got stuck in the wire, and let out a yell of pain.

'Next thing the guard is shouting: "Who goes there?" We stayed silent, while he shouted again. Silence. We knew that he was entitled to shoot after the third challenge, so when it came, we were all prodding each other to say something.

'Finally I piped up in my high-pitched voice: "*It's Cinderella, it's gone midnight and she's* pissed!"

'We were hauled before the CO the next day, and given dire warnings of what would happen to us if it occurred again. Other than that, we got away with it.'

There was one last trip to France, this time with the Americans. The Mulbury floating harbours were in use and flat-bottom boats, all very seasick-making. On arrival there wasn't even time for a cup of tea before the show started, and afterwards they travelled forty miles over potholed roads to be greeted by an extremely irate officer. 'You're late, my men have been waiting two hours.' Another show and still no tea. When that was over, Dick asked the officer where the Gang Show hut was. 'You're not staying here,' was the answer. 'You've got to move out at once, fifty miles down the road. No time for tea!'

No wonder Dick had a taste for tea after that.

Once again the lorry was their home, and with that came the problem of ten boys travelling together for hours on end with no stops when nature called.

The solution was a battered old bucket which was passed around when needed. As the lorry lurched through unmade roads and potholes, the bucket had to be emptied frequently.

On one occasion, the Cox twins were talked into 'swilling out' duty and reluctantly took hold of the bucket which was by now three-quarters full. Dick peered round the rear flap to judge the moment when the lorry would slow down and they could dispense with the contents. A railway crossing loomed up. They would have to slow down. Perfect!

At the right moment he shouted to the twins, who heaved the bucket over the near side – drenching a poor old Frenchwoman whom they hadn't seen walking along by the hedge. She was soaked from head to foot and left screaming obscenities at the top of her voice and shaking her fist at her assailants as the lorry trundled away.

Dick, hanging from the back, shouted back an apology in the only French words he knew: '*Oui! Oui!*'

As if they hadn't done enough entertaining in the show, the boys amused each other with outrageous stories and sketches whenever they had a few hours off duty. Dick's speciality was reading articles from the *News of the World*. He used as many as twenty different voices for each story, keeping the others in convulsions. One of them laughed so much he actually fell out of his bunk.

Away from the footlights they became a close-knit team of pure camaraderie. They depended on each other to get the laughs onstage and to keep up their morale offstage. They realized that if anyone stepped out of line and tried to become a prima donna, the whole essence of Ralph Reader's inspiration would fall apart. They were the Ten Musketeers, all for one and one for all. As such the Gang Show was a hit wherever it went.

Inevitably, the time came for them to be disbanded. The Chief had a quiet word and a farewell handshake with his boys. He said to each one of them in turn: 'If I ever pass by a theatre and see your name in lights, I won't pretend it was my doing. But you'll have to forgive me if I kid myself that I helped to screw in the bulbs!'

Ralph continued for many years with numerous productions, always encouraging new talent and getting the very best from his performers. He finally retired in 1974 and died in 1982. In his memoirs he noted: 'Dick's name is for ever recorded in the annals of the RAF, whose motto is *Per Ardua ad Astra* – "Through Glory to the Stars". And most surely "Through Glory with a Star – Dick Emery".'

10. It's Only Money

'I'd rather be a ham than Hamlet'

DICK TO HIS FRIENDS

As Dick came to the end of his RAF and Gang Show stories, I realized that since talking about the departure of Zelda, he had made no references to women. This was strange, as he had admitted he was 'woman mad' before the War, so I teased him and enquired whether the 'terrors of war' had put him off.

'Not so much the terrors,' he replied with a grin. 'More a lack of opportunity. Although we did "get lucky" once or twice. It's amazing what you can do on a stretcher!' His face clouded over. 'Actually, getting divorced and losing my son did slow me down a lot.' And then more brightly: 'But when I got back to London, I soon made up for lost time.'

'I bet you did,' I retorted, anticipating the next story.

Dick was finally demobbed in 1946. He had stayed on with the Gang Show proper for as long as he could and then remained with Ralph Reader in the 'Civvie Street Gang Show' at London's Stoll Theatre for the next six months. During this time he established himself as a character actor of considerable talent, which was reflected in his take-home pay of twenty-two pounds a week. He played many different parts, including a stuttering old man, a pompous officer and a toothy vicar. He was also the 'leading lady' in two lavish shows called *Tivoli Days* and *Geraldine*. He went with the company on tour to various theatres around the country, ending up at the Opera House, Blackpool.

Once again Dick became obsessed with proving himself with women. Now that survival was not uppermost in his mind, there was time to indulge his libido. Soon he met and fell in love with a glamorous singer and dancer named Irene Ansell. Still an incurable romantic, Dick was not satisfied with an affair if he thought he was 'in love'. Only marriage would do. In a matter of weeks Irene became Mrs Dick Emery number two.

They set up home together in a flat in West London, and for a short while even Bertha couldn't spoil their happiness – although she certainly tried to. Losing her only son to another woman once was bad enough, but when it happened again she was beside herself with rage, and said so at every opportunity, telling Dick that it wouldn't last and he should 'come home' and live with her.

The dreaded triangle was beginning to emerge: Dick, wife, and mother. He began to get very stressed about it, and Irene was completely out of her depth in dealing with such a complex character. To add to their problems, Dick now left the security of working with Ralph Reader to 'go it alone', but found himself without an act, not much money saved, nerves which were getting worse and confidence fading fast. This became too much of a strain on the marriage. Nine months later he was 'going home to Mother', and by their first anniversary it was all over.

In desperation, Dick channelled his energy into work. He wrote a special act for his vicar with teeth, dog collar and all. He rehearsed non-stop for a month before venturing out, as the competition was strong, with many freshly demobbed actors looking for work. They used to meet up at a pub called the Grafton in Westminster. This was the family watering hole of Jimmy Grafton, who would make his name as one of the country's leading scriptwriters, and Dick soon found himself rubbing shoulders with the likes of Harry Secombe, Frankie Howerd, Tony Hancock and his old pal from the Gang Show, Peter Sellers. Jimmy later recalled that the lads knew they were 'on the bottom rung of a slippery ladder', but they also knew fame and fortune were at the top, waiting for anyone who could hang on long enough.

With boundless enthusiasm and a determination born of not knowing where the next meal was coming from, they went on the daily slog around the West End agents, the all-powerful czars of their show-business empires without whose backing it was almost impossible for a struggling hopeful to get through the Stage Door. Dick saw it as an assault course: keep your nerve, have your script ready, get the words right – and go for it!

In the immediate post-war period, cinemas and live theatre came back into their own. People wanted to laugh. Music halls were again packed. Variety was king.

The search for work was soul-destroying. It meant climbing endless faded linoleum-covered stairs around Soho and amid the bookshops of Charing Cross Road, and sitting all day long on hard wooden chairs waiting for a call to the inner sanctum. The faces of the other hopefuls became a familiar sight as they thumbed through the *Stage* weekly newspaper looking for 'situations vacant'. Sometimes tempers flared. When an agent asked Frankie Howerd: 'What are you working in now?' the reply was a furious yell. 'Nothing! If I was working, I wouldn't be here, would I?' Needless to say, Frankie didn't get the job.

After an exhausting and usually fruitless day they were all longing to get back to the comfort of the Grafton, which became their base camp for thinking up sketches and trying out new gags on each other.

Sir Harry Secombe remembers Dick from the saloon bar: 'He was like a lot of us who met there, recently released from the services and determined to make our way in show business. We had a lot in common – and like old friends do, whenever we met subsequently, we'd take up exactly where we had left off.'

It was Harry who was among the first to spot that Dick was not a 'funny man' as such. 'He was a comic actor, and there's a world of difference. He didn't like telling jokes, though he could laugh with the best of us. He preferred anecdotes where he could slip into character – and have us in stitches.

'In my opinion he never realized his full potential as an actor, though in his sketches on TV he really did show what fine acting ability he had. People may find this hard to believe, but personally I'm sure he could have been equally successful as a dramatic actor as he was a comedian.'

But Dick plumbed for laughs. 'I'd rather be a ham than Hamlet!' he announced to the throng gathered over their pints of bitter in the saloon bar. Because money was tight, a pint would be made to last a long time.

So he did it his way, and armed with his fifteen-minute Vicar act, he landed his first job – at the Grand Theatre, Brighton. 'There were two shows a day, one a matinee, the other starting at 8.00 p.m., with three hours in between. I walked out from the wings for that first show, stared out at the audience and began the act. Two minutes later my mind went blank! It was just awful. I blanked out completely and only just managed to get myself off the stage. I don't even remember how or whether they were booing me off, or merely watching in silence.

'I couldn't bear to stay in the theatre or talk to anyone, so I headed for the Stage Door and walked out without a word. It was pouring outside and for three hours I walked around Brighton in the rain, with no idea where I was, just going over and over the lines in my head. *What had I done?* It had never happened before, however terrified I was with a performance coming up.

'I thought of running away. How could I face the rest of the cast – or the producer? But I knew that if I did that, I'd never work again.' Somehow Dick forced himself to trudge back through the rain to the Stage Door of the Grand. Once inside, he prepared for the worst, steeling himself to face the music in more ways than one. But to his astonishment (and relief) – nothing! 'No one said anything. Not the producer, nor the theatre manager, nobody! It was as if it had never happened.'

So Dick gritted his teeth again and marched out through the curtains for the evening show in his dark clerical suit and dog collar, to attempt his fifteen minutes of fame. The teeth were false and fitted over his own like tombstones gleaming in the spotlight while he went through his monologue, which took the form of a sermon, with all sorts of puns and dubious double entendres. The applause was generous, if not ecstatic. But it was enough to encourage Dick to stay on – he daren't break his contract, anyway – and somehow he got through the rest of the week.

Following that shaky start, Dick squared his shoulders and managed to get a few more jobs. A night here or a week there, often the length of the country apart. He got laughs and applause but still didn't feel satisfied with his act, although he couldn't think what to do about it. He was convinced his material should be original. He hadn't yet learned that almost nothing is truly original, only the way it is presented. His lucky break came during a week at the Chiswick Empire, where comedian Bill Lowe, who was greatly admired by Dick, saw his act.

'If I'd known he was in the audience,' Dick recalled, 'I would probably have fallen off the stage, so thank God I had no idea he was there. He came back to my dressing room after the show and discussed my act, suggesting where I could add to the character and get better laughs.' Encouraged and helped by Bill, Dick achieved more and better dates. Now his diary started looking busy, and for the first time he was able to expand some of his other characters.

By the end of 1946, Dick got his first taste of pantomime in *Cinderella* as one of the ugly sisters at a prestigious theatre in Blackpool. This was followed by the inevitable succession of summer shows, pantomime and near-starvation in between.

'I was never sure when or where the next job was coming from. Like a lot of performers, I was filled with a terrible depression when I wasn't working – and I became a bag of nerves when I was!' But in this no-win situation Dick found himself making new friends all the time.

One such acquaintance, who became a special friend, was Tony Hancock, who outshone even Dick in being a victim of his own insecurity. Tony lived in a first-floor flat in Leicester Square, two minutes from the Windmill Theatre, in a surprisingly spacious apartment for a comedian who was more often out of work than in it. The weekly rent was hard to earn, which was why, when Dick first set foot inside Tony's front door, he found no furniture whatsoever. Just a sink, a gas cooker and a loo down a gloomy passage. There wasn't even a mirror – Hancock shaved in front of the polished copper geyser.

'Where do you sleep?' Dick asked in bewilderment, his voice a hollow echo in the cavernous room. Tony pointed to the corner. 'There,' he said. But there was no bed, just a pile of newspapers. 'Fresh sheets every day, matey! And I put a coat over myself for warmth.'

Dick grinned. 'Five-star comfort, eh?'

What little food Tony could afford, he ate standing up at the mantelpiece. As they grew to know each other better, Tony would sometimes invite Dick round for breakfast. 'He would boil us a couple of eggs in his one and only pan,' Dick recalled. 'And we would eat them out of a coil of newspaper like an ice-cream cone, with one elbow nonchalantly leaning on the shelf above the gas fire. When times were really hard, we'd share an egg between us! But we never stopped talking.

Apart from showbiz gossip, we'd put the world to rights – and then plan our careers in detail, working out how we would become international stars . . .'

Tony got his big break when he was taken on at the Windmill Theatre as resident comic, a lesser-known part of its famous burlesque review. The job meant security with steady money coming in. It was a lifesaver. No more endless travelling, the bills could be paid, and he might eventually be able to afford some furniture!

The Windmill show started at nine o'clock in the morning and continued until midnight. An early audience might consist of only three people, but the seats filled up as time moved on. The girls were chosen for their beauty, and even though they were not allowed to move so much as an eyelash, they were famous for the wonderful naked tableau in which they posed. Tony confided this information to Dick after he had been working at the Windmill for a few weeks. They were sharing another stand-up breakfast at the mantelpiece in Tony's flat.

'Imagine how soul-destroying it is trying to get laughs from people who wish you weren't there. You wouldn't believe it, but when the girls go off, everyone in the audience gets out a newspaper and reads it till they come on again.' Dick shuddered to think of it. 'Why do they have comics and acts then?' he asked indignantly. 'So they can change the set. Me, I just think of the money,' replied Tony, and he took a pound out of his clip and pushed it into Dick's breast pocket. Dick protested, but to no avail. All Tony would say was: 'It's only money.'

The subject of money and how to get it was always uppermost in their minds. So Tony encouraged Dick to write to the Windmill's formidable producer Vivian Van Damm, whose name was known throughout the business as a law unto himself and whose owner was the scourge of many a hopeful who dared to step out onto that stage. Dick had nothing to lose, so he wrote off. No reply. Months passed and he forgot all about it. Then out of the blue, an envelope dropped through the letterbox at the flat in South London where he was still living with his mother. *Report here for an audition* – at 11.00 a.m. on the following Monday. Dick was so unnerved, he actually dropped the letter – and was trying to pretend it was all a mistake when Bertha picked it up and read it. 'Of course you must go!' she told him sternly. 'This is your big chance.' So off Dick went clutching his Vicar's script. He had never set foot inside the Windmill before and couldn't get Tony's terrifying description of a sea of newspapers out of his mind. So with understandable trepidation, Dick tried to swallow his nerves and reported to the Stage Door.

He remembered Harry Secombe's audition at the same theatre, having heard all about it at the Grafton pub. Harry's act was his 'shaving routine'. Rotund and jovial, he walks on, looks out at the auditorium as if staring into an invisible mirror and pretends to shave, talking to himself all the while. Of course he gets soap in his mouth, nicks his cheek and generally makes a mess of the whole thing. On first seeing it, Van Damm had hired him on the spot.

Dick had changed into this funereal suit and dog collar. He had pared his Vicar's act down to eight minutes for the audition – and eight minutes can be a very long time for a comic. He marched out onto the stage, peered into the stalls and made out row upon row of seats, empty apart from the impassive figure of Van Damm sitting silently in the fourth row. But he went for it with his toothy sermon from an imaginary pulpit – and to his surprise the impresario let him get right through his act. At the end there was a brief silence. Then Van Damm called out: 'Okay, when can you start?'

Dick phoned his mother. 'Get some meat on tick,' he told her. 'We're going to eat!'

By the time Dick successfully auditioned for the Windmill, Tony Hancock had finished his stint there, so Dick was booked to appear at once. The Windmill was a tough school and none came tougher than Vivian Van Damm – 'the Boss,' as he was known. Each show ran for six weeks, so while performing one act, Dick was expected to write and rehearse a new one ready for the changeover. Every week the Boss held auditions for new acts. All kinds of performers turned up. Comics, magicians, jugglers and singers, all resigned to being 'fillers in' between the nudes. Dick remembered one act in particular.

'I watched this magician arrive, complete with swirling cape, top hat and cane. He had three taxi loads of tricks, and unloaded them all through the Stage Door. He spent a whole hour setting up his props and finally he was ready to go through with his audition. He began with a very simple trick with his handkerchief, sliding it down inside his sleeve and was just pulling great yards of it out in a whole rainbow of colours when Van Damm shouted from the stalls: "*Thank you. Next!*" The unfortunate magician then spent another hour packing up all his gear. Then he ordered three more taxis and drove off in total dejection. Poor man, I couldn't bear to look at him.'

Dick stayed a year at the Windmill and every day gave him renewed confidence. Writing fresh material for the six-weekly change of show focused his mind. He brought new characters out of creative corners, made them flesh and blood, dreamed up anecdotes and sketches – even if it was only to face a sea of newspapers. No matter. More often than not he got through to his audience and the laughter that was music to Van Damm's ears filled the small theatre.

Although now successful in his career, Dick's personal life seemed to be going from bad to worse. He could not sustain a relationship, however hard he tried. He didn't realize what a devastating influence his mother was having. Her attitude was simple: as long as the girl was no threat to her relationship with her beloved son, no problem. But if it looked as though Dick might be getting serious, out came the talons. Her way of ruining any romance was to play one off against the other. A snide remark or a comment about her son incautiously dropped behind his back – 'Oh, sorry, dear, I shouldn't have said that, but . . .' all conspired to nip every potential romance in the bud before it had a chance to blossom. Having got her darling son back twice she was determined not to lose him again. Not knowing this, Dick blamed himself. His feelings of inadequacy grew stronger, which meant he had to prove his manhood more and more fiercely . . . until he became a legend in dressing-room gossip!

Whatever demons were after him in his own life, Dick was always keen to help a friend. A couple of months after he started at the Windmill, he was taking a breather in the street between shows one afternoon, when he bumped into Tony Hancock, whom he hadn't seen for several weeks. Tony was wearing a jacket, trousers, a tie – but no shirt! His chest gleamed bare in the afternoon sun. Under one arm he carried something wrapped up in newspaper.

After the initial embrace and backslapping, Dick said: 'Where are you off too?' Hesitantly, Hancock confessed he was trying to find someone he could borrow money from to do his laundry, including the shirt that was in the newspaper bundle.

Dick reached into his pocket and pulled out a handful of pound notes. He pressed them into his friend's hand.

'It's only money,' he said.

11. Stage Fright

'The good'uns always sweat before a race'

DICK TO LIONEL JEFFRIES

Dick had been friends with Lionel Jeffries and his wife Eileen for more than thirty years. Li, as Dick called him, and Eileen had a charming cottage near Saffron Waldon, where we often went to visit them. Sitting in their pretty garden with long cool drinks, Dick and Li would reminisce, giggling together, and keeping me in hysterics for hours. They made an unlikely couple with Dick's diminutive, dapper figure and Li's large gaunt frame crowned by the most famous bald head in the business. The conversation always started off by recalling how they had met in the mid-50s on a TV series called *Room at the Bottom*. Lionel was starring although it was his first TV show and Dick was a guest actor, by then an old hand at TV and radio.

Radio had played a major role in Dick's professional life. He got started while still at the Windmill, when he was feeling confident enough to write to the BBC and as many impresarios and producers as he thought might give him work. He had his own professional notepaper printed up with his name in the top left-hand corner, and dead centre in green capitals: COMEDIAN. He sometimes wrote on the Windmill's impressive blue notepaper if he felt that might do the trick. And one day it did.

His first five-minute spot was on *Showtime*, one of the top-rated radio variety programmes in the country. Dick recorded his act at the Aeolian Hall on 12 August 1948. It was transmitted two weeks later on 2 September at 7.30 p.m. on the *Light Programme*. He was paid ten guineas with a further eight every time it was repeated. But the most important thing was that he knew the listening figures would be in millions. The comedy circuit continued with *Variety Bandbox, ITMA*, more *Showtime* and *Henry Hall's Guest Night*. Over the next few years Dick returned frequently to *Variety Bandbox* and appeared in other popular shows such as *Music Hall, Happy-go Lucky, Variety Fanfare, Spring Salad* and *Summer Showtime*, always for the same ten-guinea fee. He also took part in *Workers' Playtime* from the Ovaltine Factory at Watford.

While he was doing all this on radio, he was still playing in summer shows and pantomimes, although now he had moved up to 'dame', still chasing women, still living at home with his mother, unless he was on tour and in 'digs', and still suffering from terrible nerves and stage fright despite gaining professional experience and confidence. At last he had worked the required twenty-eight consecutive weeks in the provinces to earn his Equity card – that a vital union membership, without which it would become increasingly difficult to work in the West End of London, on radio or later for TV.

By the summer of 1950 Dick was confident enough to agree not only to star in, but also to direct, the summer show in Ventnor, Isle of Wight. It's not uncommon for the star to direct, and requires mostly organizational skills, but Dick also had imagination and flare so the show opened to great success.

On the first day of rehearsals his eye instantly alighted on a beautiful girl in the chorus line who was able to sing and make people laugh with her bubbly humour. She bore a striking resemblance to a young Joan Crawford. Her name was Iris Tully, and Dick – mindful of 'director's perks' – made his move at once. With the blatant excuse that he wanted to wash his hair but had no hot water, he presented himself at her digs complete with shampoo and towel – and she let him in! Dick fell madly in love with Iris, and from then on they continued to see each other whenever and wherever they could.

The show was not so lucky. A sudden outbreak of polio turned the picturesque island into a virtual pariah state as far as holidaymakers were concerned. Headlines in the national papers branded it 'Polio Isle'. Swimming pools were closed, an isolation hospital was opened, iron lungs were flown in, and children queued to be given the Salk vaccine in lumps of sugar. A local journalist named Maurice Leppard, who was a cub reporter on the *County Press* based at Newport, vividly remembers the atmosphere at the time. 'There was panic in the air. People were really frightened. Holiday bookings dropped off alarmingly, and the local MP Sir Peter Macdonald called for calm. But it was no good. It was the worst summer anyone could remember.' No bookings meant empty seats at the Winter Garden. By the end of that terrible summer, three people had died, fifty-four people were paralysed and a further forty-one non-paralysed cases had been registered. By then the Dick Emery summer show had long since packed its bags and departed. In fact it had closed down at the end of the first week.

This was a blow to Dick personally, professionally and financially as he found himself back in London while everyone else was away in their summer shows. But he renewed his efforts on radio and although he didn't know it, deep inside the portals of Broadcasting House, Auntie Beeb had been watching him since his Windmill days. In the corporation's personal files there was a card which read:

DICK EMERY (comedian)

DESCRIPTION: Dark young man of 33. 5ft 6ins. Jewish-looking (exterior) in lounge suit, cap and scarf. Baritone voice.

PERFORMANCE: Patter, vocal impressions of 'auditionees'. Straight vocal finish.

TIME: Eight minutes.

EXPERIENCE: Currently Windmill. Equity. Principal comic for Tom Arnold in panto.

REMARKS: Talented and amusing, with good mike singing voice. Should prove suitable Televariety.

At that time, television was in its infancy. But the powers-that-be in BH (the BBC loves initials) were always thinking ahead, even though they couldn't have guessed how far Dick's star would rise on the small screen. When it did, Dick was ready and waiting. In fact he only had to wait until October of that year when he made his first TV appearance in a production called *The Centre Show*. He was rebooked for that show in

'51 and '52. Radio continued to play an important role. During 1951 Dick recorded fourteen shows and seventeen in '52 and '53.

In order to be available for Iris whenever she was in London, Dick moved out of his mother's home in South London and into his own flat at number 14, 171 Shaftesbury Avenue. But Iris was often away and Dick hated being alone, especially at night when what he called the 'demons' came for him, and he would be consumed by anxiety. He wrote that one morning when he woke there alone he simply lay semi-dormant, a veritable corpse, with no one to turn to for help.

I could not move, see, hear or say anything. In my head, I seemed to be looking down a long tunnel – not dark but revoltingly green! Everything hurt. My head pounded like a jackhammer and my feet felt as though they had hundreds of red-hot needles sticking into them. Even breathing was an effort.

After what seemed like hours I began to get back to normal. I managed to clamber out of bed, but I had no sense of balance and couldn't focus properly. I also felt dreadfully sick, a horrible nausea that swept over me in waves. The only thing I could do was crawl back into bed and wait for something to happen – I had two choices: either I was going to get better or I was going to die. It was as bad as that.

In the end I fell asleep. I slept round the clock and when I woke I was aching all over but I was able to face life again. But my voice had gone. It wouldn't come back for three days and I had to cancel my show, something I had never done before or ever expected to do. No voice, no singing. I just couldn't go out there and face an audience.

It happened again, more than once. Finally, I knew I had to talk to someone.

The someone was Spike Milligan, an old chum from radio and music hall days – not terribly close, but a person Dick felt he could trust. They sat in Spike's kitchen in North London, talking over a cup of tea. Dick's first words were: 'Spike, I think I'm going mad!'

Spike's retort was equally blunt. 'So,' he said. 'Join the rest of us!'

But, recognizing his friend's genuine distress, Spike softened. The zany comic who could put on the craziest act in the country, but was himself in reality a profound thinker and student of philosophy, put Dick in touch with a hypnotherapist who had helped him out in the past.

Dick was thankful for any aid he could get but thought he needed something more and eventually found himself in the consulting rooms of a Harley Street psychoanalyst, under whose care he would remain for three years.

The analyst took Dick right back through his childhood, on the tortuous trail he had bottled up ever since his father turned his back on the family, and left mother and son to fend for themselves. When the sessions finally ended and Dick felt able to face the world again without, in his words, 'throwing a wobbly', the doctor told him: 'You will go on improving slightly for a year – and after that you will become a success.'

Spike Milligan recalled those days of emotional turmoil. 'I never knew Dick well enough to make a profound analysis – I left that to the professionals. But I came nearest to helping him with his traumatic marriages, and his inner physiological stress problems for which I recommended a hypnotherapist. Success came late to him and even when he was enjoying the fruits of it, fate intervened.

'Dick confided in me how he once tried to commit suicide, when he was living alone in London and struggling to make a living. He blocked all the windows and doors of his flat with newspaper, then turned on the gas. What happened? It ran out! Dick was so poor he didn't even have a shilling for the meter!

'That was Dick – a strange but basically lovable person.'

In the midst of all this trauma, Dick started working again. For one thing, the bills had to be paid. For another, Iris Tully had moved into flat 14 in Shaftesbury Avenue, first to look after him and now to set up home together as a serious commitment, although marriage had not been mentioned. She had proved herself to be a capable actress and light comedienne, and in 1951 was understudying Cicely Courtneidge in Birmingham. Whenever the star fell ill Iris had to take over.

Dick recovered slowly, starting back with radio and theatre and then braving the TV cameras once again. *Up Spirits*, *Kaleidoscope*, *The Centre Show*, *Fast and Loose* and *Spice of Life* were some of his early TV ventures, plus featuring with Jon Pertwee and Max Wall in their popular series.

He also continued in the inevitable summer show, this time in *Dazzle* at Bognor with veteran stand-up comic Eric Ross. Dick gave credit to Eric for teaching him many of the tricks of the stand-up routine, including the dangerous game of tackling hecklers head-on with a suitable put-down that would silence the (usually well-oiled) miscreant and not cause enough offence to lose audience sympathy.

'You don't want to start a riot, son,' Eric advised his new protégé. So Dick learned that 'Last time I saw a mouth like that it had a hook in it!' was treading close to thin ice, while 'Aren't they adorable at that age?' always got a laugh and no resentment. *Dazzle* went from strength to strength and Dick was invited back to play the seaside season at Weston-super-Mare and Lowestoft in consecutive summers.

All those years later we were still sitting in Lionel Jeffries's garden listening to these tales, but it was getting cold and almost dark. As we went in for dinner, Li turned to me and said: 'That was just about the time Dick and I met on *Room at the Bottom*. We hadn't worked together before but of course I knew Dick as a very funny radio and stage comic actor. Acting on TV was a terrifying experience. We went out live with only forty-five minutes' air time and no cuts or retakes. I hated it and Dick noticed. After a couple of days he came up to me and said bluntly: "You're not enjoying this telly lark much, are you, boy?" I'd longed to talk about it to someone but an open ear was not available till then.

'Dick said: "Listen, nobody's more scared than I am, boy! Total jelly, that's what I am. In fact, I packed it in while I had a year under psychiatry. I totally lost my nerve, and my voice with it. I'm doing this to get my feet wet."

'I could hardly believe what I was hearing. This vibrant, buoyant, brilliantly talented bubble of a man was a jelly? Dick insisted: "The secret is not to show it, Li. Everyone's scared if they're talented, that is. It's like a race horse: the good 'uns always sweat before a race!" It helped knowing terror was an occupational hazard!'

By the time we were sitting at the table and Eileen was serving a delicious dinner Dick and Li started laughing again, both thinking of their favourite story of early days in TV when a lot could go very wrong. Michael Caine was the brunt of the joke. Having just landed his first role on TV, he was playing a guard in *Joan of Arc* and he had three lines to say. Dick took up the story.

'Everyone was in a state of tension because we all knew that hundreds of thousands of people would be watching us. The technicians often got all the camera movements wrong and came at you from all directions.

'Michael had to enter a room at the top of a Norman tower where they were keeping Joan of Arc, grab her by the arm and haul her out to be interrogated. He came in through an arch and was wearing one of those helmets that look like a shell casing. He knocked it on the arch as he entered and it went all lopsided on his head! He looked slightly pissed, but was too nervous to do anything about it.

'He forgot the three lines and turned to take Joan out – only to find the camera had tracked in and blocked the door. So you had this unforgettable shot of him coming right up to the lens, and saying: 'Oh bugger it!' in close up, before looking in panic for the nearest exit.

'Unfortunately this happened to be the window. So thousands of viewers saw him help Joan of Arc up onto the ledge, and jump out of a Norman tower eighty feet up!'

By this time, Dick and Li were laughing so much at the memory, they were almost under the table and crying on each other's shoulders. 'Dick makes me laugh more than anyone I know,' giggled Li, 'and I know how to tap his funny bone too. I'm always outrageously rude to him until he becomes hysterical.'

'We have a rule,' retorted Dick, 'that we insult each other at every opportunity, including really vicious attacks on each other's work – something you just don't do face-to-face in theatre. But we do it publicly, never letting on that we previously arranged to do so. People are so shocked, it's wonderful.'

They continued to giggle like mischievous schoolboys all through dinner, not to mention every other occasion I saw them together.

12. Dummy Run

'Ever-decreasing circles'

DICK IN THE FLYING BALLET

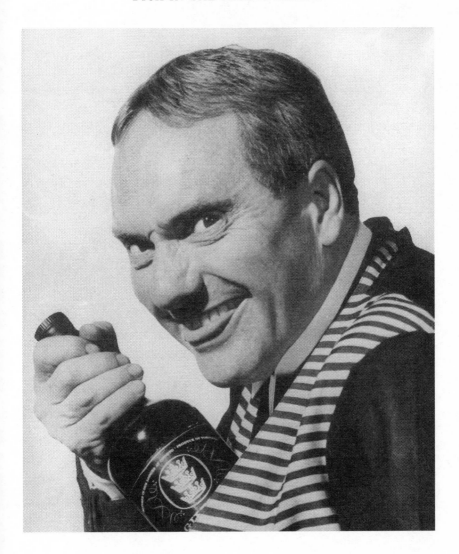

Whenever Dick spoke of Iris his voice softened and he always had something nice to remember. With her he enjoyed the only 'normal' family life he had ever known. She was aware of his two previous failed marriages and of the very strong hold his mother still tried to keep on him, so she must have been a brave woman to take him on! Not that they were a quiet couple; both of them had short fuses but a terrific sense of humour. If they couldn't laugh away their differences, the street outside their flat became a dangerous place for passers-by as cups, saucers and plates flew through open windows and doors – preceded by Dick fleeing for his life. But as they genuinely loved each other, the missiles soon stopped and they were back in each other's arms.

In April 1954, Dick came off stage at the Chiswick Empire to find Iris sitting in his dressing room waiting for him. She had some unexpected news. She was pregnant. Dick was delighted, cracked open a bottle of champagne and toasted Iris, himself and the future arrival. Six months later on 17 October, Iris duly presented him with a baby son, Nicholas. Dick was thrilled at becoming a dad again, particularly as he still had no idea of the whereabouts of his long-lost first son. He and Iris decided to get married at last, and finally tied the knot in the spring of 1955 at Holborn Register Office in central London.

With a wife not working and a son to look after, Dick felt a surge of responsibility. Iris did go back to the stage within months of Nicholas coming into the world, but only because they needed the extra income as Dick was still keeping his mother (of course).

At one point they sat down to discuss a second business away from the uncertainties of the stage, something with a dependable income. 'The only thing I'm good at,' Dick said, frowning, 'is driving. I could go back to being an instructor.' 'What a good idea,' Iris responded, somewhat to Dick's surprise. She was genuinely enthusiastic, however bizarre the idea sounded. To prove it she put her savings into a second-hand car that would start off the Dick Emery Driving School, and sat down with him to plan a schedule and work out the figures. Sadly, it never got off the ground. In the end Dick stuck with what he knew best – making people laugh, rather than having his nerves (and maybe his precious car) shredded by well-meaning learners.

Once again Dick concentrated his mind on success. Vital if his wife, son, home and mother were to survive. Bertha was as possessive as ever, and had tried every trick in the book to prevent Iris from marrying her Dickie. Now the middle-aged matriarch had relapsed into a sullen acceptance of the situation, though she made a meal out of being dependent on her son to pander to her every whim. Despite the added stress of coping with his mother, Dick was happy at home with Iris, adored his baby son – and now his career started heading into orbit. He was topping the bill at variety shows up and down the country, playing any town big enough to boast a theatre.

'Life should have been perfect,' Dick reflected sadly. 'But it was because I was successful that things started falling apart.' Iris was jealous of all the time Dick spent away from home. She knew only too well the temptations of touring and she knew Dick. She could never be quite sure that he wasn't having an affair with some girl from the chorus line in his latest show. However much Dick pleaded his undying love for her – and his eternal fidelity – she always had doubts.

The truth was that he probably loved Iris more than any woman he had ever met. But as the months passed he became more irritated by the constant accusations and questioning over where he had been and what he had been doing – and who he had been doing it with. 'I started to think: If I'm going to get blamed for something I haven't done, I might as well do something to get blamed for!' Fuelled by suspicion on the one side and resentment on the other, the marriage began to fall apart. In public they kept up appearances, and spent many hours together, attending showbiz functions and generally enjoying a lifestyle that was getting better as Dick's star ascended and the post-war economy started to boom.

Dick's act now included several new characters, plus songs and a stooge, the stooge in question being a 'feed' planted in the audience who would shout 'rubbish' at every opportunity. This (rehearsed) heckler was one that Dick could insult at will, and he went at it with gusto, leaving the audience in hysterics as the pair traded gibes throughout the act. It was at this point that Dick came into contact with an entertainer who scaled fewer inches in his socks than himself – which may have been a plus factor in his book. Charlie Drake was a baby-faced comic who looked as if he had just fallen out of his pram, and spoke in a voice to prove it. 'Hello, my darlings' became the catchphrase that caught on throughout the nation, and you would hear it repeated from building sites to street markets in the same hilarious high falsetto.

They met at a TV show and hit it off at once. Dick invited Charlie to become his stooge – and for months to come, his high-pitched screech would make itself heard in theatres across the land as Dick took his show everywhere, and little Charlie with it, shouting the odds from the back of the stalls.

Together they worked out a grand climax to the act. Dick finally appeared to lose patience and invited his tormentor onto the stage. 'You think you're so clever – come up here and prove it!' Which Charlie duly did. After more insults two pairs of boxing gloves were produced and the two hammered the daylights out of each other in a mock ring battle, ending with both of them flat on their backs as the curtain rang down to tumultuous applause. 'The greatest exponent of a boxing match onstage was Norman Wisdom,' admitted Dick. 'The difference being that Norman was by himself – boxing his own shadow! At the end he would get knocked out and do an amazing pratfall, literally appearing to be knocked off his feet. The fellow was made of India rubber!' Norman had actually been a boxing champ in the British Army, so perhaps he had the edge on Dick and Charlie.

When Charlie was honoured with *This is Your Life* in 1961, Dick paid him a tribute. In return, Charlie said of Dick: 'An actor can speak with the words of angels, but unless he does his work with love it is just surface gloss. Dick Emery loved his work.'

Radio continued to keep Dick active with twenty-one shows in 1954. They included a number of surprise appearances in *The Goon Show*, standing in for Harry Secombe when the jovial Welshman was away on other contracts. 'Dick was the only one mad enough and capable enough to pick up scripts and carry on with no fuss,' said a producer at the time. He became close friends with Peter Sellers, his old wartime comrade from the Gang Show days.

In 1955 Dick starred with Laurie Lupino Lane in a riotous variety show at the Adelphi Theatre in the Strand. Variety? It was more like anarchy, with Laurie's zany genius inherited from his father, the legendary Lupino Lane, to provide an unforgettable night of knock-about comedy, slapstick and 'slosh' sketches (custard pies and wet mops in abundance) to send the audience home in stitches.

Laurie had been born in 1922, the scion of a theatrical dynasty that went back to the 1500s. He had first appeared at the age of eight in a children's theatre company run by his uncle, Stanley Lupino, alongside his cousin Ida Lupino. The glamorous Ida became a Hollywood star in the 40s. She referred to herself rather unkindly, and certainly unjustly, as 'the poor man's Bette Davis', before carving out a second career for herself as virtually the only woman director working in America in the 50s.

Laurie meanwhile teamed up with another music hall great, George Truzzi, a member of a famous circus family, and together they revived the art of slapstick and took it to new heights – or depths, depending on which end of the custard pie you were on. So Dick was soon zooming out of the wings with a dozen policemen, helmets askew, singing their hearts out as they 'flew' like huge insects around the stage and out into the audience, often reaching as far as the dress circle. The boys in blue were the stars of Kirby's Flying Ballet, the show-stopper that did indeed bring the show to its rousing finale. This arresting spectacle was achieved by means of a harness which was fitted between the legs, round the waist and up over the shoulders. Floating out over the stalls 'in ever-decreasing circles', seeing the open mouths and staring eyes gaping up at them, was a memory Dick recalled with relish.

'As usual, there was very little time between the sketches to scramble into the harness. Apart from Joe Kirby's own boys, the leading members of the cast joined them to take the final bow.

'More than once the harness would slip – and you'd see us hanging there, half upside-down, suspended over the stage with lop-sided grins of agony and tears and sweat pouring down our faces . . . but still trying to sing, in unusually high voices, depending on where the harness was stuck! None of us would ever forget that show.'

Now came another milestone in Dick's life. In 1956 he met a ventriloquist called Peter Brough – and his career jumped a further rung up the ladder. Peter was a year younger than Dick and, with his suave, bow-tied dummy, Archie Andrews had become known as Britain's answer to America's Edgar Bergen (father of Candace) and Charlie McCarthy (Charlie being the dummy).

Educating Archie ran throughout the 50s and hit the ratings as one of the most popular shows on radio. A ventriloquist on radio? How could it be? It seems impossible that such a bizarre idea could attract an audience of millions, but it did – and Peter Brough and Archie Andrews became a national institution.

With the comic vitriol running through the veins of writers Sid Colin, Eric Sykes and Ronald Wolfe, the urbane Archie became a human being who could destroy people with a curl of his tongue – even if the voice was that of nice upstanding Mr Brough.

Archie would refer to his lord and master simply as 'Brough'. The trick was to bring in celebrities as support, who duly took Archie's insults straight on the chin knowing that a huge rapt audience had tuned in every week to hear the hilarious banter. Names like Max Bygraves, Hattie Jacques, Julie Andrews, Jerry Desmonde (later to suffer untold indignities as Norman Wisdom's straight man), Tony Hancock, Alfred Marks, Warren Mitchell, Bruce Forsyth and Sid James all queued up to be insulted.

Dick not only became a regular on the programme, but it brought his name to millions every week – compared with a seaside show, however popular, that would only be seen by thousands at best. He was paid twenty-one pounds a time, plus twenty-pound repeat fees. The scripts were brilliant. They led to bigger things, with a live show becoming the number one draw in theatres throughout the country: *'Educating Archie, Radio's Top Line Family Feature'*. They moved into TV, but with markedly less success, and Peter would eventually become a prosperous businessman and finally retire to the peace and quiet of the actors' residential home in Denville Hall, Buckinghamshire.

With new friends in the business around him, and a dummy adding to the fun and games, the only enemies Dick had now were his own 'demons' which still wouldn't leave him in peace. His marriage was floundering badly, with his mother fuelling the flames of annoyance into hatred. Once more the triangle was inevitably in place.

13. In Love . . . Again

'It was the dog collar that got me'

DICK ON WIFE NUMBER FOUR

'At least this business gives one the chance to escape,' Dick drawled lazily from the depths of a sun lounger on an exotic beach in Fiji. We had 'escaped' from England a week before, where every national paper, it seemed, was carrying a sensationalized story about Dick and me. The proverbial had hit the fan, when our (by then) affair had been discovered by the Press. It was very lucky that Dick had a tour booked for New Zealand and Australia, with time for a holiday in Fiji before he started. After the trauma of 'going public', with all its ramifications, lying on a beach in complete anonymity was a healing process – and for Dick, so was confession.

He was appalled at the number of times he found himself leaving someone and starting up with another. He agonized over Zelda and Irene, then told me in detail how sad he was when everything went wrong for him and Iris, which meant he wasn't around as much as he would have liked to see baby Nicholas grow up.

'But,' he groaned in despair, 'I don't seem to be able to help it. I really try to make things work, but they won't – and then along comes someone else and I just know "with that person life will be perfect". Of course it never is.' He leant over and patted me with a hot sandy hand. Obviously trying not to hurt my feelings, he added: 'But I always live in hope!'

For myself, I hoped and prayed we would be perfect together. But before I could dwell on that, Dick had started telling me about his split from Iris.

In 1956 his 'escape' was to star in the summer show in Lowestoft, Norfolk, where he was surrounded by good acts, beautiful dancers and a soubrette who immediately caught his eye – a soubrette being the singer-dancer who leads the chorus. Eighteen-year-old Victoria Chambers was a 'little doll' (his words), perky and sparkling, standing only an inch or two taller than him. He was certainly intrigued, not least by Vicky's offbeat fashion sense. The first time he saw her offstage she was wearing a red leather studded dog's collar around her slim neck. Dick was spellbound and found her 'stunningly irresistible'. Apparently she didn't resist him either. They went out for a drink, and Dick learnt all about her.

To his delight he found she came from a famous show-business family herself. Vicky's parents were Hal and Vera Chambers, who ran a stationery shop in Seaview on the Isle of Wight. That was the day job. They were talented entertainers in their own right, with Hal a wizard on the keyboard and also Dickie Valentine's regular pianist for many successful years.

'Seaview?' said Dick thoughtfully. He knew it well. Vicky couldn't have guessed that the Isle of Wight had become one of his favourite stamping grounds. 'They're not part of Moody's Minstrels, by any chance?' Moody's Minstrels were an informal group of artistes named in homage to the local entertainment manager Don Moody, who was responsible for booking many of the artistes for the local summer season. All were known to be ready and willing to perform for the amiable Don whenever he asked.

'Yes, they are! How on earth did you know that?' Vicky was open-mouthed in astonishment.

'Because I am too.' Dick grinned.

Dick had made the Isle of Wight almost a second home, travelling over on the ferry from Portsmouth every Sunday whenever he could during the summer, courtesy of 'the Don's' friendly persuasion.

He would do his show at two theatres on the same night, before catching the last ferry back to the mainland! First house would be at the Shanklin Theatre, then Dick would nip into a waiting taxi and race three miles up the coast road to the Sandown Pavilion. He would occupy the entire second half, which sometimes meant a longer interval for the waiting audience if the coastal traffic was heavy. Both Sunday shows inevitably were sell-outs.

Writer and broadcaster John Hannam, who has a regular slot on the local radio station, recalled: 'Dick was a bit of a legend over here. He was enormously popular and had a great following. In turn he loved the Isle of Wight, where he had made many friends.' John remembers dropping into the Chambers' stationery store in Seaview's High Street to buy some envelopes, and spotting an oddly familiar figure serving behind the counter. That looks like Dick Emery, he thought. Then moments later: Strewth, it *is* Dick Emery!

Part of Dick's pursuit of the luscious Vicky was to materialize in Seaview, getting to know the parents and impress them – and his quarry – by giving a hand in the shop . . . even if he did spend more time signing autographs than ringing up the cash register.

When the summer was over, Dick and Victoria went their separate ways, with mutual regret. As a gifted pianist, Vicky played the piano in hotels and restaurants up and down the country in between theatre dates. So they were both busy, and had little opportunity to meet. Dick had made no secret of his marriage, and although he couldn't get Vicky out of his mind he returned to Iris and his baby son – to try again!

'God, how I tried,' he would moan to close friends, unburdening his guilt and insecurity on sympathetic ears. Actor and comedian Freddie Sales would later recall: 'Dick bared his soul to me often, admitting the turmoil that was in his mind and how depressed he would become when he considered some of the things he had done. Part of the problem was the miles that would often separate him – both from his loved ones and from his friends.'

But Ronnie Barker remembered a more positive side of Dick, from the days when they were both struggling for recognition. Ronnie recalled: 'I always admired Dick's skill and technique. I first saw him playing the dame in pantomime in the late 40s, and even then he was truly an actor's comedian.

'I never ceased to be amazed at the clarity and definition of his characters. Not one of them ever drifted into another one. Each was crisply and accurately portrayed. Above all, they were really *funny*.

'One did not think: Oh, how clever! or How true! when watching one of his old men lurching about. Or: What accurate observation, as his reverend man of the cloth drank tea with raised eyebrows and crooked finger. One was too busy laughing.'

But there wasn't much to laugh about in Dick's life as he tried to forget Vicky and concentrate his efforts on his wife and child. Iris now had good cause for her doubts and jealousy. Dick phoned Vicky often, even from his own home when he thought the coast was clear, 'just for a chat'. Of course Iris didn't see it like that, and after eighteen tortuous months, they had their final confrontation. It ended with Dick moving out to rent a tiny flat in Sloane Square, where he persuaded Vicky to join him. Bertha didn't know whether to be delighted at the split or even more jealous of the new competition.

The public never knew and the Press never got a whisper of it. 'If they had,' Dick conjectured, 'that would have been it for me. Imagine the headlines: "Top Comic Abandons Wife and Baby for Teenage Temptress". Or words to that effect. They'd have crucified me.'

But after six months in the flat together, Dick's conscience started troubling him even more than his loins. After a sleepless night of heart-to-heart searching with Vicky, he decided he must go back to being a husband to Iris and a father to Nicholas. Victoria left the flat, found a job as an assistant with Mary Quant's fashion house in Knightsbridge and rented a bachelor-girl pad for herself in Richmond. Dick, meantime, bought a 'family house' and moved his wife and son in to give it yet another try. However, Victoria could not forget Dick, and no matter how hard he tried, he again could not get her out of his mind. Six weeks later he was back in Sloane Square and Vicky was with him.

Plagued by guilt and consumed by lust, Dick penned this remarkable and revealing account of the inner nightmare he was enduring. It was among the items in the suitcase of treasures he gave me shortly before he died. He told me he had written it at that time, but it could in fact have applied to any one of his disastrous marriage break-ups.

The pounding in my ears, the sudden spasm of agony between my shoulder blades. Thoughts that churn my brain in dizzy whirls. The fibres of my flesh that burn with need brought on by thoughts impossible to destroy.

Please stop, lest I become a stumbling wreck and perish in the depths of my despair. God, give me strength to crest the waves of my discontent. Give me the strength that I may face the rest of my life with courage, truth and love, or I may sink forever in the loneliness of my tortured soul.

Love is so elusive and sometimes so difficult to recognize. Unbelievably, love can hide itself in the depths of hatred and despair. Hidden, locked away as if never to be able to find a key to bring it back unscarred, untainted by the hatreds and harsh words that hurt and cut deep into one's very soul.

The answer is truth.

What do we know of truth? That black is black and white is white? Yes, but that is only one part of it. To find love again, to relive it as if new – then it is necessary to turn inwards and seek the truth from inside.

It is no easy task when this moment arrives, for then you are face to face with yourself and most of us are loath to look for fear of what we might discover. To be appalled at the creature we see. Vain, selfish, contemptuous, pompous, unaware of the unhappiness heaped on others. Impervious to pleas for mercy and understanding.

No! Don't turn away, don't avoid the unpleasant! For this is what they call the moment of truth. How many of us can face it? How many of us can answer truthfully?

We are what we are because of our unawareness. We clumsily wreck people's lives. Have we been fair? No . . . then we must ask ourselves why, and have the courage to face the facts. The facts inside. The true facts. For if we answer them honestly then awareness, not of self but of others, will come.

Time will cease to be because life will be held at a standstill and then one can begin to feel and even see the love that has been waiting so deep beneath the surface of hatred and hypocrisy.

'Don't let that moment go by. Hold it tenderly as you would a wounded bird, and nurse it into a glorious love, uncluttered by petty things. A love that transcends all, human or otherwise.

And then the two of you will have found Paradise. Here on earth, not hereafter, but now.

On the beach in Fiji, of course, I had not seen this anguished writing. But just hearing him recall the pitiful comings and goings between two people he cared for, trying not to hurt either and hurting both more as a result, I pitied him, and them, and myself, for by then I had also suffered from his indecision.

But that, I hoped, was behind us.

125

14. Still Climbing

'Tone it down a bit'

BBC BOSS TO DICK

Dick's success in *Educating Archie* led him to be asked to co-star in a Granada TV series called *Two's Company*. This proved to be a disaster and almost cost him his delicate grasp on self-confidence. It did nothing to endear him to TV's top brass either. But he hung on and got another opportunity in 1958 with ABC TV's production *After Hours*. This was not only more successful, but also where he met Michael Bentine for the first time. Michael was full of ideas and when the TV series was over he asked Dick, Clive Dunn and Ray Barnet among others to join him in a tour of a comedy play he'd written called *Don't Shoot, We're English*.

Clive, later to become one of the stalwarts of *Dad's Army* ('They don't like it up 'em!'), remembers it well. 'We did the tour, heading for the West End with any luck, but with mixed audience response and reviews along the way. By the time we reached Hull, we were in a state of depression. One afternoon Dick, Mike and I wandered around the streets and found ourselves in a "pull up" café for lorry drivers, where we sat in a group drinking mugs of tea and gloomily looking into the future.

'Suddenly the silence was shattered by a local, who called across: "If you lads are looking for work, they need a commissionaire at the hotel up the road!" We looked at each other, Dick, Mike and me – and our day was made.'

They didn't make it to the West End. Undeterred, Michael kept writing and thinking up outlandish plots. He had begun his stage career with a wild hairstyle and beard, a mad professor with a mind-boggling variety of props to help his act. Everyday items like a sink plunger, a broken chair, a shooting stick and an inflated inner tube could generate laughs, and Bentine proved it. And with Sellers, Secombe and Milligan in tow, the *Goon Show* was born.

Dick never missed an opportunity to sing Michael's praises. 'When you're at your lowest ebb you find out who your friends are,' he often repeated. Michael proved to be a good friend. In 1960 he was given his own TV series called *It's a Square World* and wrote Dick into as many episodes as possible, where he became a huge success. Michael was pleased to remember how Dick always mentioned *Square World* when speaking of his rise to fame. 'So few people give credit to those who have helped them to stardom. Dick was one of the few, and I shall never forget him for that.'

Also in 1960 Dick fulfilled a long-standing ambition – to break into movies. The lure of the big screen beckoned and finally his old mate Peter Sellers helped him achieve his goal – in the bizarre and virtually indescribable comedy *The Mukkinese Battle Horn*. Dick was afraid he got this part through his friendship with Peter rather than on merit. Peter was having a bad time with his private life, and had phoned Dick in the middle of the night for advice and comfort. Without hesitation, Dick jumped into his car and roared to the rescue, staying with Peter for the rest of the night.

By daybreak, when Peter felt better, Dick went home. A few days later he received a call from the studios with an offer of work. He never turned work down, but when he saw Peter he had a quiet word. 'Friendship needs no repayment.' Peter could hardly believe someone wanted to help him without being rewarded.

In the same year, Dick made another film that was directed by Lewis Gilbert, a jokey black and white saga about life on a searchlight battery during World War Two, called *Light Up the Sky*. Dick found himself in the company of a roll-call of lively talent, all anxious to prove themselves for the big cameras and the huge 'brute' arc lights that lit up the night sky in a little Surrey village called, unexpectedly, Normandy. '*Vive l'Anglais!*' murmured Dick, remembering his own landing on the beaches. On a thin budget, British Lion had rented an old cricket pavilion to recreate the camp base, and turned the pitch into a remarkably realistic airfield. Since Biggin Hill and some other wartime airfields weren't much bigger, it probably wasn't too hard.

It was an early film for Lewis Gilbert, who would go onto become a distinguished veteran of the business, with a vast cross-section of contrasting themes under his belt. From war films like *Reach for the Sky*, *Carve Her Name with Pride* and *Sink the Bismark!* to romantic comedies like *Alfie*, and *Educating Rita* and the musical *Stepping Out*, he also directed three James Bond epics: *You Only Live Twice*, *The Spy who Loved Me* and *Moonraker*. Lewis Gilbert carved his own name with pride in cinema's hall of fame.

In *Light Up the Sky* Dick played a postman delivering mail to the boys at the battery. He worked for just three days and only had six lines, but he made the most of them.

'Dick was enormously enthusiastic, and always brightened the place up the moment he walked through the door,' Gilbert recalled. 'He was just great fun to have around and was always full of beans. The one thing I remember about him was just how much he really loved acting. Seeing him on TV later in his marvellous drag outfits, it always struck me as weird because there was no one less female than Dick Emery!'

The early 60s were a busy time for Dick. On TV he was in the *Ted Ray* shows, plus *Panorama* (no relation to the later investigative news programme) and *Make Mine Music*. On radio it was *Variety Playhouse*, *Funny Side Up*, *London Lights*, *It's a Fair Cop* and more merciless ribbing from *Educating Archie*.

All this activity and hard work had not gone to waste. BBC memoranda reveal how, unknown to Dick, the top brass had discussed for some time the possibility of signing him to an exclusive contract. One dated 9 October 1962 from the formidable Tom Sloan, Head of Light Entertainment, had spelled it out: *'Subject, Dick Emery: Exclusive Contract . . . with the intention of launching him as the star of a revue-type series. One-year option, possibly extend in the future. Suggested fee: three hundred guineas a show.'* On that memo someone had scribbled in pen: *'Try £250.'*

Early in 1963, Dick was summoned to the BBC for a meeting with Sloan. 'I was shaking with excitement and nerves,' Dick recalled of that momentous day that really did change his life. 'We shook hands – and then without further niceties Tom came straight to the point. *"How would you like your own show?"*

'Would I? Is the Pope a Catholic? I said *yes* almost before he'd finished speaking.'

Then came the questions. Could Dick handle an entire show under his own name, or would he prefer to be the 'star guest' every week in a big production number? Sloan spelled out the potential pitfalls when you carried the whole thing on your shoulders: the buck stopped there. If things went wrong, there would be no one else to carry the can. Dick was undaunted. Somehow his nerves had vanished, to be replaced by a quiet confidence that assuaged the top man's doubts. 'I welcome the challenge,' he said levelly. They got down to brass tacks. 'How would you visualize the show?' Sloan asked. Dick answered at once. 'Comedy sketches within a storyline,' he replied. 'And I'd want to include as many of my characters as possible.' But the big man frowned across his desk. 'Too ambitious,' he said. 'You'll have to tone it down a bit.'

Fair enough. Dick knew better than to argue at that early stage. *Get your foot in the door, then take it from there*, had always been his motto, drummed into him at an early age. So they settled for quick comedy sketches, interspersed with street interviews where Dick was dressed in a variety of guises being interviewed by a long-suffering reporter, and backed up by guest singers and a bevy of glamorous dancers. The producer would be Ernest Maxim, a seasoned campaigner with top variety shows like *Morecambe and Wise* on his impressive list of credits.

Contracts were swiftly drawn up, but there was the usual delay of several weeks before the cameras rolled. During this time, two major hiccups had to be sorted out. One was the title. The top BBC brass felt that although Dick was a big name in the business, perhaps he wasn't quite big enough to hold the show on his own. They proposed calling it *The Dick Emery Theatre* and Dick had to go along with it. The Press gave him good coverage. A new star was about to be born within the BBC ranks, with his own series and a whole ladder of opportunity rising ahead.

The second hiccup was more serious. Up to that point Dick had been going through agents and managers hiring and firing like the proverbial knife through butter. At last he had settled with an agent named Michael Sullivan. Eager to make sure his client was working, Sullivan had signed Dick into a forthcoming West End play, a comedy called *Luv*

My favourite picture of Dick.

Callen and Emery -
Dick's parents in the act
that frightened him
as a young boy.

Dick aged three.

Bertha, Dick's mum.

Laurie, Dick's dad.

Dick aged eighteen,
with the Silver Songsters.

Dick with Zelda,
his first wife.

The Gang's all here! Ralph Reader is third from the right, middle row,
Dick is on the end of the middle row, right, and the Cox twins are sitting.

The Gang Show on stage. Dick is Vera Thin, in a polka-dot dress.

Dick as an early panto dame.

Dick's second wife, Irene.

Dick's piano sketch at the Windmill.

WINDMILL (WE NEVER CLOSED) THEATRE
PICCADILLY CIRCUS

The Goon Show, 1953. *Right to left*: Peter Sellers, Dick,
Phil Burn, Spike Milligan.

Educating Archie. Dick with ventriloquist Peter Brough and Irene Handl.

With Michael Bentine in *It's a Square World*.

The Big Job. Dick with Sid James and Lance Percival.

Dick's third wife, Iris.

Dick with his fourth wife, Vicky.

Bertha continued to
influence Dick's life.

Dick was a runaway success as
Queen Ermyntrude in *Puss In Boots*.

Dick with Joan Sims on
The Dick Emery Show
(top left).

Dick with June Whitfield.
Christmas Special, BBC.

On one of his many
hospital visits.

On a wing and a prayer. Dick 'wing walks' for a dare.

Summer Season, and Dick is in his element.

'Mandy' has a painful landing in *Ooh, You Are Awful*.

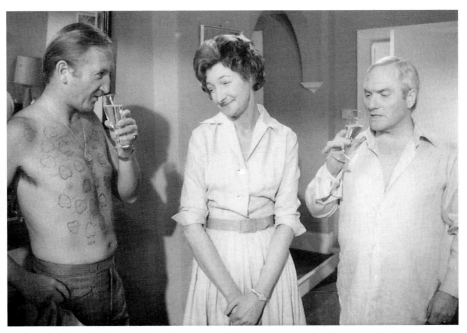

With Pat Coombes and Ronnie Fraser in *Ooh, You Are Awful*.

Dick salutes the brains behind his show: writers John Singer (*left*)
and John Warren, with producer Colin Charman.

With Roy Kinnear and Mickey Rooney.

Dick in Paris with
Margaret Thomas.

Dick with his mum in her
twilight years.

Dick's reunion with Number One son, Gilbert.

Dick with his second son Nicholas.

Dick's fifth wife, Josephine.

Dick with his daughter Eliza, and third son Michael.

High roller!
The proud owner
with his Rolls Royce.

A kiss before Dick
buzzes Perth in his
Tiger Moth.

Keep-fit Dick.

Prospecting for gold with
Dick Down Under.

The last picture of us taken together and the only one at Lowlands, our final
Shepperton home. This was taken about four months before he died.

which co-starred George Cooper and the husky-voiced Fenella Fielding. The setting was New York. Dick and Co were supposed to play denizens of Brooklyn, complete with accents, and although they found it almost impossible they persevered with rehearsals. The BBC caught wind of this, and the balloon went up approximately a month before the opening date. Dick received a terse message to present himself in front of Mr Sloan and explain how he thought he could possibly be in two places – Lime Grove studios and the West End – at the same time.

Dick stuttered and stammered and tried to explain that his agent had gone ahead with the play 'feeling sure it wouldn't clash with my show'. Tom Sloan, with thunder darkening his brow, gave him the ultimatum. *Us or them?* There was no contest. Dick ordered his agent to get him out of the play. But as days passed in haggle and negotiation, the BBC lost patience – and dropped *The Dick Emery Theatre* from its schedule. The newspapers got hold of the story and the headlines shouted: 'BBC Axe Dick Emery' . . . and many more words to that effect.

Dick was appalled. He didn't want to lose his whole TV future for the sake of a play that was at best 'doubtful', at worst a born loser. Behind the scenes, Sullivan was desperately trying to mend fences, but the chilly memos still on file reflect the feelings at TV Centre.

Unknown to Dick or his agent, a sharp letter dated 24 April 1963 from Mr S.J. de Lotbiniere, who held the lofty title of CPSTV (Controller of Programme Services, TV) went out to C,TelA (Controllers, Television Administration), Assistant Solicitor, HPC (Head of Programme Contracts), HABTel (Head of Artists Bookings Television) and HLEGTel (Head of Light Entertainment Group Television).

It stated: 'Dick Emery is having difficulty in meeting rehearsal and recording dates due to rival engagements.

'This whole incident has been a very serious one for the BBC, but even now it is difficult to know how in future to provide really effectively against such a combination of stupidity and sharp practice.'

Eventually the play went ahead without Dick and he was allowed back into the BBC fold. The ironic twist to all this was that the furore catapulted him into the headlines and into the public domain. The BBC decided to call his upcoming series *The Dick Emery Show* after all.

They paid him three hundred pounds a time (guineas now being outdated, even as show-business currency) and the following year his fee rose to four hundred pounds. This show gave birth to Dick's characters as we now know them and provided him with the catchphrase by which he would soon be known internationally: '*Ooh, you are awful – but I like you!*'

15. In Character

'Clucking away'

LAMPWICK

I had the chance to observe Dick 'in character' from a very close perspective. It was fascinating to watch the transformation, whether he was being made up by a professional while recording for TV and film, or slapping it on for himself in the theatre dressing room. Apart from the obvious changes from male, female, straight, gay, young and old, there were hundreds of subtle variations that would probably go unnoticed by the public as they were absorbed into the whole image. The change that appealed to me most was in his hands. I'm sure if I could have seen only his hands, I would always have known which character he was playing. I don't think he did this consciously; it just happened as the character came to life.

That show-business sage Donald Zec, who filled columns for the *Daily Mirror* with his own special brand of wit and humour, once observed about Dick: 'Deep inside his densely populated mind lurk some of the most preposterous – but highly recognizable – characters that ever pimped, pouted or solicited their way into universal favour. Those who disagree with me can probably be counted on the fingers of one hand.'

Dick put it more simply. 'A lot of nonsense is talked about the business of characterization. It's simply a matter of observing and relating.' He gave an enlightened account of how he slid seamlessly into the character. 'As I sit in the make-up chair, I go through my lines. It is during this time that the transition takes place. There's nothing profound about this, the ability comes from long familiarity with the character.

'Imagine living and working alongside the same person year after year! You get to know their every mannerism, every twitch. That's how it is with my characters.'

During the course of Dick's career he must have played hundreds of different characters, but perhaps there were about a dozen best loved by the public and therefore most often portrayed by Dick. Or was it the other way round? The roll-call mostly included:

MANDY: The buxom blonde who gave him his best-known catchphrase: 'Ooh, you are awful – but I like you!'

THE VICAR: Buck teeth, dog collar and evil twinkle.

LAMPWICK: Clucking, patriotic old soldier.

HETTIE: Man-starved spinster.

COLLEGE: Gentleman tramp.

TON-UP BOY: Motorbike lout.

CLARENCE: Outrageous gay with the catchphrase: 'Hello, Honky Tonks – how are you?'

THE DUCHESS: More royal than the Queen.

CLIVE THE SPORTING GENT: A British Cad.

THE INVENTOR: Unsuccessful DIY enthusiast.

BOVVER BOY: Criminal juvenile, Dad's little helper with the catchphrase: 'Dad, I've got it wrong again!'

HEN-PECKED HUSBAND: Always trying to dispose of his wife.

I could go on with the German Officer, the Flying Ace and so many more – and even if you have only seen one *Dick Emery Show* you will recognize at least several of these characters.

Dick's own favourite was Lampwick, a doddering but proud relic of World War One. He felt a kinship in the essential 'Britishness' of the old warrior. 'If he saw an injustice, he wouldn't hesitate to put his fists up and have a go, clucking away all the while and choking in an attempt to give vent to his indignation!

'He represented that will to live and stubborn refusal to submit to the limitations of old age, which is the bravest way to cope with a fact of life that's going to happen to you anyway. He and his like are priceless.

'In the chair it takes half an hour to transform me into Lampwick. They rumple my hair and whiten me around the eyes with a spot of shading on the cheeks and forehead to make my face look older and more lined. On go the moustache and specs, and as I watch myself in the mirror being physically transformed into Lampwick and hear myself speak his lines, there I am – Lampwick himself!'

One of Dick's favourite sketches was when Lampwick overhears his daughter Lily (Helen Fraser) and son-in-law Ernie (Victor Madden) discussing how to get rid of 'the old thing' because he's past it. The audience and Lampwick think they are talking about him and only at the end do we realize they've been discussing the family budgie!

Dick loved the opportunity to combine pathos and humour, and in the following sketch Lampwick had the perfect mixture. The scene is set in the sitting room of the Lampwick household. Lily is sitting on the settee placidly knitting. Ernie is reading a newspaper. Propped against the wall is a large, embroidered British Legion banner. The domestic peace is suddenly shattered by a blast on a cracked bugle and the sound of tramping feet from upstairs. The door bursts open and Lampwick marches in. He is wearing a bowler hat, his best blue suit with wing collar, and his campaign medals from the '14–18 War are pinned across his chest.

LAMPWICK: Lef' right, lef' right. Halt! Dismiss!

ERNIE: Oh my gawd! What do you think you're playing at?

LAMPWICK: You're talking to an Old Contemptible—

ERNIE: That's a good word for you.

LAMPWICK: I never saw you in the trenches.

ERNIE: I tried to lie about my age, but my nappies fell down.

LILY: Now stop it, you two!

LAMPWICK: If they'd handed out white feathers in the last lot, he'd
have looked like a flaming Leghorn chicken.

ERNIE: That's a lie! I had a very good war record.

LAMPWICK: Yes, I've heard it. Vera Lynn singing 'We'll Meet Again'.

ERNIE: Talk about home sweet home. There's no living with him.

LAMPWICK: (*pathetically*) That's right, have a go at a poor defenceless old man on his day of glory.

ERNIE: Glory? What are you talking about? You march down the road carrying that silly flag and go straight into the pub. Ten minutes marching and four hours boozing – that's your day of glory.

LAMPWICK: That silly flag, as you call it, is the banner of the Starch Green branch of the British Legion. And me, Lance Bombardier James Maynard Kitchener Lampwick, being the oldest serving member, has the honour of carrying the banner.

ERNIE: Oh, you do what you like with it!

LAMPWICK: If I did what I like with it, you'd find yourself in the bedroom without having to walk upstairs!

The scripts were the brainchild of John Warren and John Singer, who had been writing 'quickie' sketches for Dick since before *The Dick Emery Show* started and were on the same wavelength as him about his brand of comedy.

In that first crucial year, when the public were getting used to a rampaging new talent in their midst, Dick's sharp eye for impersonation and alert ear for speech rhythms and dialects had to be contained in case it ran amok. His characters seemed to be multiplying by the minute and his energy knew no bounds. One of his sketches was titled *The Will to Fail*, in which Dick played a down-and-out called Charlie, whose costume details on the call sheet were listed as: '*Striped collarless shirt, trousers with braces, heavy boots, socks with holes and ragged sweater*'. Behind the scenes, various bills presented to the programme accountants gave only tantalizing clues as to what made up the early shows. For instance, a fee of ten shillings and sixpence was paid for the hire of a No Parking sign, while a Colonel Whitehead, Chief Ranger of Wimbledon Common, received five guineas for his services, whatever they might have been. Props for other sketches included: '*One park bench, six slender saplings seven feet tall, 1lb of acrylic fibre to go in trees, two fog machines.*' And for a library scene: '*Two dozen various library books, two trays of authentic library books, six pencils . . .*' plus: '*one pint of shrimps.*'

Dick rarely had a major star on this show because he really didn't need them. His characters were 'stars' in themselves. What he did need, and steadily amassed, was an army of supporting actors, among whom were such names as Joan Sims, Pat Coombs, Mary Millar, Rex Garner and Michael Balfour, with the Cliff Adams Singers completing the show. No one quite knew what they were in for when they signed the contract, only that it was prime-time TV with an audience of millions, so they would go along with nearly anything. A letter to Michael Balfour at his home in Kingston-upon-Thames from the producer John Street only hinted at what lay ahead for the actor: '*Please find the script of the Limping Grenadier for* The Dick Emery Show, *in which we would like you to play the part of the first man . . .*' The Limping Grenadier? One only has to imagine the Changing of the Guard, courtesy of Dick and his scriptwriters, to laugh out loud. Or, same producer to same actor: '*I am enclosing a script for a sketch entitled Who Shall we have for Dinner? – We thought you might perhaps like to play the part of the Native Chief.*'

Second only to Lampwick, another early favourite was Ton-Up Boy because he enabled Dick to indulge his passion for motorbikes and talk about them non-stop. 'I always loved mechanical things. I spent my childhood studying the performances of British motorbikes at the TT races. At that time our country's true glory and achievement lay in the noise and smell of machines like the Norton . . .

'I am passionately interested in motorcycles. The sensation of riding headlong into the wind on a powerful machine which obeys your least touch is an exhilarating one and remains the core of the attraction of motorcycling, though fashions in gear and bikes may come and go. I get a surge of pleasure just from watching a rider roar off on his motorbike. As long as he's not causing trouble or endangering others, I wish him luck.' And he revealed: 'Most of the bikes used in the series were mine!'

Ton-Up Boy was easy for Dick. 'I didn't need a lot of make-up – except for the wig! I wore a military helmet, goggles and the black leathers adorned with chains – oh, and a white scarf around my neck.

There had to be a cigarette hanging out of the corner of my mouth to round it all off.'

Dick had found the inspiration for this early character in the bikers he met during his months at trials, races, clubs and cafés around the country. 'I watched them, and I was amazed at their dedication to their machines.' He remembered an occasion when he opened the National Motorcycle Exhibition and was escorted through a coffee bar crammed with leather-clad bikers. He felt a sense of threat as he saw a group of Hell's Angels staring at him from one corner – 'glaring balefully at me as I signed autographs'. Dick's solution was to march up and get heavily involved in an argument about which bike was going to win which race that season, and how to spot a Harley-Davidson owner in a crowd. He won them over with his genuine enthusiasm, and by the time he left he had a few more fans into the bargain.

'The Ton-Up Boy has been part of my family from the word go. He is happy-go-lucky, full of the kind of jokes he might have picked up from the Chapter's last gathering, and above all dedicated to his machine. I'm not sure that I invented him – I just spotted him out there and invited him into the show!'

INTERVIEWER: Excuse me, sir.

TON-UP BOY: Yeah, son?

INTERVIEWER: Tell me, do you find there's a strong community spirit in your neighbourhood?

TON-UP BOY: Fantastic, that's what it is, fantastic. Take what we've done for Charlie the window cleaner. He fell off the ladder and broke his arm. There he was, poor old soul, wearing 'imself out trying to carry on one-handed.

INTERVIEWER: Oh, what a shame.

TON-UP BOY: Yeah, he just wouldn't stop work. So us lads stepped in and helped him out.

INTERVIEWER: You mean, you cleaned the windows for him?

TON-UP BOY: Nah. We broke his other arm.

The reviews became ecstatic. James Thomas of the *Daily Express*, a father figure among TV critics, noted:

Dick Emery's new series has brought a much-needed freshness to weekend television. His first show for the BBC again proved his inventiveness and ability to use all the tricks in the medium to produce laughter. His flair for character comedy is unique. He can play anything from a chatty blonde to a decrepit butler, and his writers John Warren and John Singer provide him with material which in anyone else's hands would appear 'camp' – a word from which Emery miraculously steers away.

Even when Dick was playing a woman he managed to be female rather than camp, as with his 'frustrated spinster', Hettie.

'She was loosely based on a middle-aged secretary in my producer's office,' Dick remembered with an affectionate smile. 'She wore huge blue upswept butterfly-wing glasses with diamanté frames, and long pleated skirts. I added a wig and one of those pink see-through blouses that were then in fashion. The way I visualized her and brought her into the "family" was to make her vulnerable and even a little pathetic. It was all to do with movement and posture – the way she clutches her bag as though it were likely to be snatched from her at any moment makes her vulnerability palpable. And the way her shoulders droop and her rapid, nervous gait bring out the pathos in her.' When approached by the interviewer, as she is in so many sketches, Hettie 'becomes a very tense little woman, suddenly aware that she is the centre of attention. She reduces everything to her obsession with finding a man and gets quite carried away.'

INTERVIEWER: Excuse me, madam.

HETTIE: Miss.

INTERVIEWER: Miss. Do you believe that some men are better than others?

HETTIE: I don't know. I've never had the chance to find out. Are you married? I'm looking for a nice young man . . .

And she jumps onto the unsuspecting interviewer.

Another product to flower in this fertile field was Clive, the Sporting Gent. Dick warned: 'Never buy a car from this man, or anything else for that matter. He is the genuine British cad. He is identified by his loudly checked jacket, jaunty bow tie and thin, well-trimmed moustache, and is usually to be found in smart bars, drinking shorts – which he never buys himself if he can help it.

'He regales all and sundry with rude jokes, jests about "the wife" and boasts about his Club, but is careful not to identify it. I like to think he's the outcast black sheep of a well-to-do family.'

Dick actually based the Sporting Gent on an RAF entertainments officer he encountered during the War. It was the day the Gang Show, filled with trepidation, flew in over the Normandy coast to land behind the recently taken beaches. 'We were still shaking in our boots when this chap came up and, greatly concerned, asked where the girls were. We could hear the gunfire across the field and bombs going off in the distance. To be asked about girls at that particular moment was bizarre, to say the least! We informed him that we played the girls' roles – to which he gave a nervous "Ha-ha-ha" guffaw which later became the Sporting Gent's trademark laugh. In fact, I thought he was so good that I tried him out on those Gang Show troops. So the Sporting Gent made his debut on a makeshift stage on the back of a lorry.'

Dick was always hoping to do more than just sketches, so the following 'epic' appealed to him and the public alike.

SCENE: *An empty first-class railway compartment. Peter, a man in his early forties, appears in the corridor. He is carrying a small suitcase. He is followed by Helen, an attractive woman in her early thirties. She also carries a suitcase.*

PETER: Here we are, darling. (*He puts their suitcases up on the rack, then closes the door. They both sit down. He grabs her hand and tries to kiss her. She turns her face away.*)

HELEN: Please, Peter, you must give me time to adjust. After all, it's not every day I run away from my husband.

PETER: I know, old girl, I feel a bit shaky myself. I've never left the wife before.

HELEN: But it had to be, didn't it, darling? It was purgatory living next door to you and being unable to touch you.

PETER: It was worse for me seeing your underwear on the line every Monday morning.

HELEN: We must take our happiness while we can. The only thing that worries me is Clive. I know he'll be broken up. I only hope he doesn't . . . do something silly.

PETER: There, there, darling.

Dick Emery appears in the corridor, dressed as Clive the Sporting Gent, in a loud check hacking jacket. He is followed by Angela, another attractive, well-dressed woman. She is carrying two suitcases and a bag of golf clubs. Clive glances into the compartment and opens the door.

CLIVE: Here we are, sweetheart. Shove 'em on the rack, old thing. (*He watches Angela struggle with the cases.*) Well done. (*They sit opposite the others, looking at each other fondly and holding hands. Peter and Helen stare at them in shocked recognition.*)

PETER: Angela!

ANGELA: (*turning in horror*) Peter!

HELEN: Clive!

CLIVE: Hell!

PETER: What the devil are you doing with my wife?

CLIVE: And I might ask you the same.

PETER: If you want to know, old man, we're running away together.

CLIVE: You rotten swine.

PETER: Well, what about you and Angela?

CLIVE: I'm a rotten swine too, I suppose.

PETER: You don't mean that you too . . .?

ANGELA: I'm leaving you, Peter . . . for Clive.

HELEN: Angela, how could you? My best friend!

CLIVE: That's rich. Sitting there practically seducing her husband.

HELEN: That's different. We love each other.

CLIVE: How long have you two been carrying on?

PETER: Well, if you must know – about six months.

CLIVE: (*triumphantly*) Ha! Gotcha! We've been at it for eight months, haven't we, old girl?

PETER: You rotter! Do you mean to say you two have been . . . you know?

CLIVE: Yes.

ANGELA: Certainly not.

CLIVE: Yes, certainly not. Tell you one thing. I'll lay you six to four you two haven't . . . er . . . you know?

HELEN: What do you mean?

CLIVE: Well, if I know you, darling, it's either 'Don't be so disgusting' or 'Can't you see I'm reading?'

PETER: I find this whole thing highly embarrassing. The least you could do is find another compartment.

A ticket inspector appears in the corridor.

CLIVE: I don't see why we should. We're perfectly comfortable here.

The inspector opens the door.

HELEN: You always were a selfish, unreasonable brute.

CLIVE: As a wife, dear, you were a flaming disaster.

PETER: How dare you speak to her like that. When you've lived with my wife for a few months you'll realize that Helen is a perfect treasure.

ANGELA: And she'll find that as a husband you're a perfect bore.

The inspector has been watching these exchanges with some interest.

INSPECTOR: Can I see your tickets, please?

PETER: (*producing two tickets immediately*) Here you are.

The inspector clips the tickets and turns to Clive.

CLIVE: Sorry, old chap, we nearly missed the train. I didn't have time to buy tickets.

INSPECTOR: Where are you going to, sir?

CLIVE: Bournemouth.

PETER: You rotten creep, so are we.

HELEN: Not the Cranley Arms?

CLIVE: (*cheerfully*) That's right, old thing. Where we spent our honeymoon. (*Helen bursts into tears. Peter puts an arm around her shoulders.*) I'll never forget that night. I want to warn you, old boy, the walls are so thin you have to oil the bedsprings before you start the old nonsense.

PETER: (*savagely*) You unutterable cad.

INSPECTOR: That'll be five pounds, sir, please.

CLIVE: (*peering into his wallet*) Oh lor'. I completely forgot to go to the bank. (*To Helen*) You haven't got a few quid, have you, darling?

HELEN: (*falling into her familiar role of wife*) I don't think so, dear. No. Peter?

PETER: I'm afraid I'm a bit short myself. Angela?

ANGELA: (*producing notes from her bag*) Here you are, darling.

PETER: Thanks, poppet. (*He hands them to the inspector.*) Here you are, gorgeous . . . I mean, inspector.

INSPECTOR: I only hope you're all going to wait 'till you get to

Bournemouth . . . otherwise I'll draw the blinds. (*He exits, tut-tutting.*)

HELEN: (*producing an envelope from her handbag*) I was going to post this to you, Clive. It's my farewell letter.

CLIVE: Oh, that's damn decent of you, old girl. (*He also produces a letter.*) I've got one for you. Might as well save the stamp.

ANGELA: (*handing over an envelope*) I've written one to you too, Peter.

PETER: (*passing a letter to Angela*) Thanks. Here's yours.

CLIVE: Excuse me.

PETER: Excuse me.

All four sit back, open their letters and start to read. There is silence for several beats. Clive starts to chuckle and then laughs out loud.

CLIVE: Good Lord, so you knew all the time?

HELEN: About what, darling?

CLIVE: About the blonde who works at the library.

HELEN: Well, I got rather suspicious when you went to change your books twice a week and always came back with *Marriage for Beginners*.

CLIVE: Damn it all, darling, having lived with you for ten years I had to refresh my memory.

HELEN: (*to Angela*) You see what you've let yourself in for?

ANGELA: Well, you needn't think you're the only other woman in Peter's life.

CLIVE: No. Knowing that blighter, I doubt if you're in the top ten.

PETER: (*waving his letter angrily at Angela*) What the hell do you mean? I think more of the Golf Club than I do of you?

ANGELA: Well, so you did. Until I made you give it up.

148

Clive stares at Angela in horror and turns to Peter.

CLIVE: She made you give it up? Golf? Good God! I'm surprised you didn't leave her years ago.

PETER: Yes. When we moved in next door to you, she took one look at that damn great garden and bang went my weekends.

CLIVE: You poor old chap. Look here, I feel absolutely rotten. I had no idea you were a brother golfer. I'd never have tried it on with your missus if I'd known.

ANGELA: Clive!

PETER: Apology accepted, old man.

CLIVE: After all, I'm Club Captain this year.

PETER: I say! I'm terribly sorry to have put you in this embarrassing position . . . Skipper.

HELEN: Peter!

CLIVE: That's all right, old boy. But I don't want to give those old elephant-trousered bags in the Ladies' section something else to gnash their false choppers over.

PETER: Oh right, right! By the way, what's your handicap?

CLIVE: Nine.

ANGELA: Clive?

PETER: Me, too.

HELEN: Peter!

CLIVE: Have you ever played Bournemouth? It's a cracking course. Look here, we could have a damn good weekend's golf.

PETER: (*eagerly*) I could borrow some clubs—

CLIVE: And stay out at the Golf Club.

HELEN: What about us?

CLIVE: Sorry, old girl. All that late night hanky-panky plays havoc with one's swing. Come on, Peter old boy, let's go and find a drink. (*They go out.*) No, the first is a rather long dog-leg left. I usually play out to the right . . .

They disappear. The girls look at each other and burst into loud tears.

No wonder that after this a *Radio Times* critic found himself asking: 'The man himself seems such a mixture, an all-sorts box of conflicting tensions that jiggles madly around until you wonder if there *is* a real Dick Emery . . .'

16. Behind the Scenes

'I'm looking for a nice young man . . .'

HETTIE

When Dick and I moved into our flat in St John's Wood, there was a mass of decorating and refitting to be done. Never content with second best, Dick wanted everything to be brand new and perfect. This included the kitchen, which was tiny. Five feet by six feet at the most, with two doors and a window. Dick instructed the workmen to install every conceivable gadget and appliance that he could think of, and as a result we were left with a space in the centre just big enough for us to stand in together as long as we didn't move. It looked wonderful even if it wasn't entirely practical, and we took it in turns to go and stand in it until laughter overtook us and we sat on the living-room carpet (the chairs hadn't arrived yet) and giggled until the tears poured down our cheeks.

'Have you any idea,' Dick wheezed at me, 'how many kitchens I've installed in my life?'

It took me a minute to understand what he meant. Dick had been a nomad all his life, married five times, and had moved house goodness knows how often. He must indeed have set up a lot of kitchens. I looked at him wide-eyed and was relieved to see him grinning. 'You'd think I'd have got it right by now,' he hissed, as we were once again convulsed with laughter.

One of Dick's kitchens was in a house in Thames Ditton which he bought as a twenty-first birthday present for Victoria, when he had convinced himself that she was the answer to all his problems. But even this didn't last, and after six reasonably happy months, Victoria was packed off to London and Dick installed Iris and son Nicholas. It says something about Dick's strength of character that his women allowed themselves to be pushed around (and I include myself in this). But he had a way of explaining things. He made his position so clear and seem so logical that no matter how outrageous his demands, none of us had the sense to refuse!

Although Dick really did love Iris their relationship was too volatile, and only weeks later Dick left her again and returned to London in search of Victoria. He found her and moved in. Another kitchen?

As far as Dick's professional life was concerned, in public opinion he could do no wrong. Behind the scenes things didn't always go quite so smoothly. Several producers came and went. Charles Chilton took the reins for *Emery at Large* in 1965, while names like John Dyas, James Gilbert and Ridley Scott – later to become a major movie director with blockbusters like *Alien* – could be found behind the control panel on Dick's shows for TV or radio.

But the most influential person at this critical time in Dick's career was that enthusiastic comedy writer, actor and director Ernest Maxim. Stocky, immaculately dressed in sports jacket and trousers with a crease you could cut your finger on, Ernest came under the Dick Emery flag in 1966 and stayed there for four riotous years, during which the show hit a peak and never looked back.

Ernest had just the right blend of humour and quiet authority to give Dick the confidence he needed. 'Dick was a very funny man,' Ernest recalled. 'But the truth is that he was a great comedy and emotional actor. Think of all the characters he played – most of them would get big laughs, but there was pathos behind many of them too. To me a comic is a man who sells his own personality, like a Bob Monkhouse or a Bob Hope, and gets laughs that way. Dick got his laughs out of creating characters. Dick could stand up and tell gags if he had to, but that wasn't his forte. He wasn't comfortable. But he could do what the others couldn't, and that was to get lost in a character that you actually believed. Audiences not only laughed at them, but loved them for what they were.'

Like Dick, Ernest had greasepaint in his blood. Starting out, he claimed, as a 'blacked-up pianist in the *Kentucky Minstrels* at the age of six'. Adding: 'They fired me at nine, telling my mum and dad that I was all washed up in the business! I think the trouble was that I was precocious instead of cute.' Such a minor setback failed to deter the child prodigy. Dick knew of Ernest's track record and asked him if he could take over the show.

From the start, Ernest sensed Dick's insecurity. He played his man cautiously, like a fisherman with a particularly slippery catch at the end of his line. They agreed to meet before rehearsals for the first show – 'So that I can find out what makes you tick,' said Ernest. 'And where you want to be in a year's time.' That was Ernest, forward thinking. It appealed to Dick, and a bond of trust began to be forged between them.

Dick confessed: 'The truth is, I don't think I've quite found my niche in comedy.'

That was a shaker and came out of the blue. Ernest recalled: 'I couldn't believe I'd heard him say that. *The Dick Emery Show* was high in the ratings, if not yet number one. I tried to come to terms with it and told him: "It should be easy for you. For a start, you're a very emotional person. If you start to tell me a sad story you'll actually cry as you tell it." Which was true. He did, and often so did his listeners.

'Dick could touch a chord with everyone. Underneath all that surface play-acting was a genuinely affectionate man. I told him: "You're a comedy actor, Dick. But when you're playing them, you look to me as if you're hiding behind these characters because there's no Dick Emery in them, even though we can recognize your face in them. You've got to bring forth your own personality and be part of them yourself." "What do you mean?" Dick asked. "Think about it. Take old Lampwick. You should look on him as your own grandfather, an old-timer who's not quite all there but is still part of your family, so your flesh and blood will come through. I don't want you hiding behind a pantomime figure."

'Dick was fascinated. "Cor!" was his first word. Then: "I never thought of it like that. Okay, I'll have a go!"'

Ernest and Dick delved into the characters, and Ernest's first suggestion that: 'Lampwick had to be his grandfather who has become the senile old man of the family who thinks he knows everything' appealed to Dick, so he worked on it for days before the start of the new series. He changed the pace and played it that much slower, and in Ernest's words '*became* his own doddery old granddad'.

Although most of Dick's energy was focused on perfecting his TV show in 1962, he managed to squeeze in an appearance in a small-budget British comedy film with the riveting title of *Mrs Gibbons' Boys*. The film's story was woven around a widow, played by the inimitable Kathleen Harrison, who is trying desperately to marry again for the sake of her three sons – who are all convicts. A cast of enthusiastic supporting actors lined up to help the fun along, headed by John Le Mesurier, David Lodge (last seen passing Dick in the demob parade), Lionel Jeffries, Milo O'Shea and the shapely figure of Diana Dors, who provided the glamour (and much of the box-office appeal) as Britain's own golden girl of the screen.

One critic described the film as an 'unattractive farce with clod-hopping characters and too much slapstick'. Dick, aware that you can't win 'em all, clodhopped gamely with the rest and from this uninspired experience an unexpected friendship was forged and was to be proved years later.

Diana Dors had little to do with Dick on the actual film, but twelve years later she was dramatically struck down with meningitis and was in hospital for several weeks. She recalled what happened. 'We had not been really close friends. But when Dick heard of my sudden illness, and not even knowing the true extent of it, he rode over to my house on his motorbike with a bunch of flowers tied on the back. He was the only one out of all my acting friends actually to come over in person to find out how I was. I never forgot what he did.'

That same year, Dick had a small part in another film with his old mate Peter Sellers, who was the star. *The Wrong Arm of the Law* was a crime caper with Peter leading a bunch of London gangsters, including Dick, who offer Scotland Yard a temporary truce while they see off a load of Australian interlopers invading their manor. It was well received and still occasionally pops up on daytime television.

Dick even found time to be a guest star on several other TV shows for the BBC. Among them were *Comedy Playhouse*, *The Great Quilow*, *Several Faces of J.D.*, *The Good Old Days*, *Wednesday Magazine*, *Play Your Hunch* and *The Singing Summers*. On radio, in which he loved to experiment with new voices, he recorded fourteen shows in 1963, among them *Music Hall*, *London Lights* and *Showtime*.

Amid all this success, fate did deal Dick a rough hand with that series for Granada TV called *Two's Company*, the other half of the duo being the ebullient Canadian comedienne Libby Morris. Audience figures never got off the ground and the show was axed after one series. Dick – being Dick – thought he would never work again. But for both of them it was just one door slamming shut, with plenty ahead along the corridor waiting to be opened. But still, always a chastening experience, and Dick never forgot the fragility of fame.

By Christmas 1962 Dick had achieved enough status to star in pantomime at the 'Holy Grail of Entertainment', the London Palladium.

The panto was *Puss in Boots*, and Dick was Puss. Which of course gave rise to a lot of ribald comments, most of them unrepeatable. The cast included Frankie Vaughan, Jimmy Edwards, Joan Regan, Mike and Bernie Winters and dancer Gillian Lynne, later to become Britain's top show-business choreographer.

But there were unexpected problems. The normally amiable Frankie Vaughan was not used to working with a gaggle of comics of the calibre of Emery, Edwards, Winters and Co.

'It was a wonderful cast, but Frankie just did not have the experience to handle us,' Dick recalled. After all, they were early days in the heart-throb singer's career. 'The first row erupted after Frankie thought Jimmy Edwards had upstaged him during the performance – which he probably had. There was a big yelling match backstage afterwards.

'The next night, he thought it was *me* who was doing the upstaging, when in fact I was doing no such thing. Mind you, I suppose you can always be upstaged by a pantomime cat! After the show I got a summons from Mr Matthews, the stage manager, to go to Frankie's dressing room.

'I had no idea what was in store until Frankie burst out with a stream of invective and a tirade of insults. I'd never been shouted at like that – not even during the War. At the end of it, I just stood there, white-faced and speechless. Finally I found the words to choke out: "Frankie, I love you. I wouldn't upstage you for anything."

'There was a long silence while we stared at each other. Then, having got his feelings off his chest, Frankie grabbed me and hugged me. "Sorry, Dick!" he said. "Please forgive me. I was wrong." He was ashamed of his outburst, but it cleared the air for the rest of the run and from that moment we were friends for life. Frankie was big enough to sit down with me a few days later and admit he had learned a valuable lesson about the business: *never stand on your high horse!*'

On the personal front, Dick was still suffering from indecision and divided loyalties. He went to visit his baby son in Thames Ditton as often as he could, laden down with expensive presents to appease his guilt. He tried to keep his mother happy, although Bertha never wasted time in jumping into a bad situation and making it worse. She played everyone off against each other and demanded constant attention from Dick, even when he was filming all day and doing a theatre show at night.

It was just as well that Dick was earning good money, as his responsibilities were increasing. He now had financial care of his mother, Iris and Nicholas and Vicky. He had bought Vicky a boutique with a nice big flat above it in Cobham, Surrey, where she could satisfy her flair for clothes and they could live together when he wasn't away working. They were getting on so well that Dick started to think of marriage again, but Iris wouldn't even discuss divorce. A few weeks later Vicky found she was pregnant and marriage became more urgent, but Iris stood firm so wedding bells were out of the question. Instead, Victoria changed her name by deed poll to Emery – and when Dick's third son Michael was born, he really believed himself to be happy at last.

But not for long. Soon his 'demons' were back with a vengeance and he felt as if he were literally being torn apart.

Hoping to be comforted and set straight, he headed back to his psychiatrist, only to be told: 'You're too serious and you're working too hard.' True enough on both counts – but where was the solution?

'Listen,' the analyst said patiently. 'These kinds of things are never all one-sided. You're taking too much of the guilt on yourself. Give yourself a chance – go out and chat up a few pretty girls!'

That kind of advice seemed to be like pouring petrol on a fire to put out the flames. 'I already do that,' said Dick.

'Um,' said the shrink, looking thoughtful. Then: 'All right, try something you don't do – something exciting and adventurous.'

17. Wings At Last

'You can't park that thing here!'

PITCHFORK-WAVING FARMER TO DICK

Dick left his psychiatrist and went away to think about what could possibly be exciting and adventurous enough to take his mind off his problems. As he was driving around rather aimlessly a poster caught his eye. It was advertising flying lessons with a glamorous girl laughing from the cockpit.

'If she can do it, so can I,' Dick told himself, and enrolled for flying lessons at Fairoaks, conveniently sited near Cobham in Surrey.

'In the beginning I was petrified,' he admitted later. 'I scared myself so much that each time I found I was still alive when I got back to the ground I swore I would never go up again. There was no beautiful blonde waiting to teach me, but I still forced myself to turn up for the next lesson. Soon the sheer enjoyment of being up there above the clouds and feeling the freedom of flying outweighed the terror.'

Dick learned to fly in the open cockpit of a Tiger Moth, like a relic from a World War One movie. 'This was true flying, and once I'd mastered the ground checks and basic straight and level flying, take-off and banking turns, I was full of confidence, a modern-day Biggles of the air!

'The worst moment in those early days was when the instructor decided it was time for me to get myself into – and out of – a spin. It was very strange, that first experience. You become disorientated and think you're pointing into the sky, when really you're diving head-first into the ground!

'The first time I did it, I managed to land the plane, walk unsteadily away and just make it behind the hangar to be sick all over the grass!

'The next obstacle is to know where you are when the ground is just a tiny patchwork quilt fifteen hundred feet below. The instructor demanded: "Right, do you know where you are?" He wasn't too pleased when I replied weakly: "In a plane . . ." But I learned how to keep an eye open for landmarks, how to read a map, watch for other aircraft, talk on the radio and check the dials – all at the same time.'

After eleven hours, Dick was ready to go solo. On a sunny spring morning, he sat alone in the cockpit outside the hangar at Fairoaks, suddenly feeling very vulnerable and unsure of himself. 'I went through the ground checks twice, just to be certain that the flaps were working. Noted the petrol and oil gauges. Everything was okay. When I couldn't put off the big moment any longer, I got clearance from the control tower and taxied out onto the tarmac.

'Then it was up, up and away – soaring into clear blue sky. Wonderful elation, total freedom, pure joy! Suddenly I was on my own, filled with confidence, doing steep turns and slow, luxurious rolls . . .

'I just flew and flew, overcome with euphoria. Then, after what seemed hours, I thought: It's time to go home. I peered over the side and didn't recognize a thing! I flew on and still nothing. No familiar landmark. I'd fallen into the old trap of forgetting to check my compass reading because I'd been enjoying myself so much.

'I started to feel the first twinge of panic. Then – thank God! There in the distance was the outline of Guildford Cathedral, and the landscape fell into place like a jigsaw puzzle. I headed for home in relief.'

The landing was bouncy but the plane and Dick remained intact. The instructor was waiting. 'Rather a long time up there, weren't you?' he said. 'Was everything okay?'

'Sorry, Chief,' Dick responded. 'I just got carried away. But it was wonderful.' He just hoped he didn't look as pale as he felt.

The instructor eyed him closely, then nodded and gave him a grin. 'Congratulations,' he said. 'It's time for your exam.'

Dick was ready to attempt his pilot's licence. It meant passing all the actual flying tests, including recovery from the dreaded spin, and also flying across country with certain map references, landing at various air strips and returning to base within a given time limit.

Dick took off in the Tiger Moth. The fields and villages of Surrey passed serenely below his wings and all went well for the first half hour. Perhaps too well. Dick described to me what happened:

'Well, I managed to misjudge the distance between two airfields and found I'd run low on petrol. I just about crawled to the landing strip, only to be told there was no petrol there. I knew I'd never make it to the next stage, so what could I do? In a panic and in full flying gear and goggles, I rushed out into the country lanes and flagged down the first car that came along, an old Morris Minor that trundled up and came to a reluctant stop.

'"I've run out of petrol! Can you help me?" I gasped out.

'"Where's your car?" asked the bewildered driver.

'"It's not a car – it's that plane." I gestured furiously at the Tiger Moth, which was looking very lonely on its own at the edge of the field.

'"All right. Hop in."'

He was a local pig farmer and he saw the humour of the situation. When he realized who his distraught passenger was, he not only took Dick to the nearest garage a mile down the road, but took him all the way back again with a couple of cans of petrol swishing about on the back seat.

Dick took his address, thanked him profusely and promised to send him tickets to the show. He poured the petrol into the fuel tank before bouncing off down the grassy air strip with a final wave to his saviour. Somehow he made it to the next port of call, refuelled and was back at base with minutes to spare.

'Luckily I had a tail wind,' he told me. 'But it was a close call.' That was Dick, living on the edge yet again.

But now he was Captain R. Emery and proud of it. To celebrate he bought himself his own plane. He had enough in the bank to afford a Miles Magister, paying out a hundred pounds for the single-engined craft with its open cockpit.

Eric Sykes recalled the pranks they got up to. They had met in the *Educating Archie* days and became firm friends after Dick was invited to join Eric on his own radio show. 'We took up flying together – I had a Tiger Moth, Dick was in his monoplane of unknown origin,' said Eric. 'We would head for Guildford and have mock dogfights over the city, like Snoopy and the Red Baron!'

Somehow they got away with it without being arrested. 'If the good folk of Guildford had realized who was up there doing mad things above their heads,' said Eric with a reminiscent grin, 'they wouldn't have been staring up – they'd have been cowering in their cellars!'

Dick never did anything by halves. Once he set his sights on a goal, he was never satisfied until he had achieved it. Now he was into planes. He sold his Miles Magister and invested in a Tiger Moth, joining the Tiger Club to put the first of scores of flying hours under his helmet. He would work out later that in fact he flew seven hundred flying hours before a heart condition grounded him and stopped him from flying solo.

However, before that happened he bought (and sold) a second Tiger Moth, two Cessnas, a Turbulent and a Cherokee. To improve his flying, Dick also purchased a 'Links Trainer', a full-size mock-up cockpit complete with dashboard and dials wired up to simulate any flying condition he might encounter 'up there'.

'I trained myself for the instrument-rating exam, which I passed with flying colours,' he reported with justifiable pride. 'It meant I was licensed to fly in bad weather with poor visibility, relying solely on my instruments to know where I was heading and to tell me if I was climbing, diving or going straight and level.

'After that I felt confident enough to fly myself to wherever I was appearing. I have to confess it didn't always work out the way I intended . . . One day I set off from Surrey to fly up to Manchester for a concert that night. Just north of Birmingham the weather closed in, and the cloud cover ahead was only three hundred feet above ground level. The usual flight path for light aircraft is fifteen hundred feet or above, so I knew I wasn't going to make it. I put down at the nearest airfield, phoned for a taxi and took a two hundred-mile trip to the theatre. What with another taxi back the next day, you could say it became a rather expensive concert!'

A few weeks later, more drama. Flying over Dartmoor on the way to a date in the West Country, Dick suddenly realized his fuel gauge was reading uncomfortably close to zero. This time there was no airfield to help him out. He searched the ground for the nearest flat space, spotted a likely looking field and was zooming in when at the last minute he saw the entire field was criss-crossed with wires for the crop.

'Somehow I brought the nose up in time to hedge-hop into the next field and found myself bumping along through a load of turnips. Next thing, up rushed an irate farmer waving a pitchfork!

'He was yelling and shouting: "You can't park that thing here. This is private property!" It must have been like something out of a *Carry On* film. I convinced him I couldn't move "this thing 'ere", until I got some fuel. We ended up with the farmer giving me a lift on his tractor to a petrol station – and yet again I was still in my flying suit and goggles! It was getting to be a habit.'

Another time, Dick was playing Blackpool for the summer season, where on a whim he bought himself a Cessna. Three years went by, and Dick's manager received a phone call out of the blue.

A voice said: 'What do you want to do about this plane?'

'What plane?'

The man on the other end said: 'Dick Emery bought this Cessna and it's still in the hangar. He hasn't touched it.'

The manager spoke to Dick, who told him: 'Oh yes, I did buy a plane but I forgot all about it. Tell the guy to sell it.'

Dick had paid eighteen thousand pounds for it and never climbed into the cockpit. He said the man could have it for fifteen, and he'd cut his losses. His manager rang back and said: 'It's okay, he doesn't want it. You can have it for fifteen thousand pounds.'

The other fellow said: 'You don't understand. The plane is only worth eight grand and the hangar charges are eleven!' In the end the man kept the plane and Dick had to send him another couple of grand!

Unrepentant, Dick continued to fly to his show venues while Victoria occupied herself by designing her own collections for her boutique, which was proving very successful, and at the same time looking after baby Michael.

One day Dick suggested flying over to the Isle of Wight to visit her parents. The weather looked good and they set off in a carefree mood. They had been over the sea for an hour, when suddenly they were enveloped in a bank of dense low cloud which ended only two hundred feet above the waves. Dick turned pale as he remembered: 'We'd have hit the Isle of Wight before we saw it!'

'Is everything all right?' asked Victoria, clutching the baby and wondering just how low Dick was going to fly.

'Yes, yes,' he reassured her. 'But I don't like the look of this weather much; I think we'll head for home.' He sounded cool and confident and landed them safely at Fairoaks, but his knees were knocking when he helped a white-faced Victoria from the plane.

Not many people escaped 'going for a spin' with Dick. Agents, managers, directors, friends and family all got their turn, and it could be as worrying for those on the ground as for those in the air.

Ernest Maxim remembered one Sunday when they were due to start a fresh series of *The Dick Emery Show* next day. He opened his newspaper over the breakfast table – and froze. A headline read: 'Dick Emery in Air Crash'!

The producer still shakes his head in disbelief as he recalls the story. 'It was a small, late paragraph and the details were very sketchy. It didn't even say anything about his injuries. In a panic I dialled Dick's number – and he answered. "Dick, I can't believe I'm hearing your voice. The air crash – what on earth happened?" "Oh that!" Dick said casually. "It happened yesterday. I was flying the Moth over the South Downs. It was a lovely sunny day and I was peering over the side at the scenery. I spotted an open-air party going on in someone's garden so I thought I'd go down and have a look. It was a wedding with everyone dressed in morning suits and summer dresses with a big marquee at the end of the garden.

'"I got down to one hundred feet and I could see this lovely table laid out with sandwiches, trifles and champagne. I could even make out the cake and the colours of the icing!

'"I was so engrossed by then that when I looked up I was heading straight for the tent! It was too late to pull up and fly over it and I could see daylight on the far side – so I made a snap decision and flew right through the tent and out the other side!

'"I took a pole away but managed to get through and land in the next field. Nobody was hurt, thank God, but they all raced out like startled rabbits and surrounded the plane. I had a lot of explaining to do – but in the end they were all wanting my autograph and even asked me to join the party!"

'Which, of course, Dick duly did.'

Captain Emery's favourite saying on flying was: 'There are bold pilots and there are old pilots, but there are no old bold pilots.' So perhaps he was lucky to survive his flying days!

Despite the vagaries of the English weather, Dick found time between the fog and rain to join the Experimental Flying Group in Biggin Hill, the legendary wartime Battle of Britain airfield in Kent, to indulge himself in aerobatics and stunts. One of the more bizarre efforts saw him dressed as a cat (complete with whiskers and tail) at the controls of his Tiger to promote his pantomime *Puss in Boots* at the Palladium. The result: headlines and publicity all round, and a definite plus for Puss.

If anyone still doubts that Dick had a maverick streak in him, they should look no further than a June evening in the mid-70s. Dick and his good friend Lionel Jeffries were watching the 1933 musical *Flying Down to Rio*, the screen classic which starred Fred Astaire, Ginger Rogers and Dolores del Rio. They had enjoyed a good dinner at the Jeffries' home with Victoria and Lionel's wife Eileen, and were sitting around watching the old black and white movie on television.

The toe-tapping story of a dance band making whoopee in Rio de Janeiro appealed to Dick – particularly the electrifying finale with chorus girls dancing on the wings of biplanes high in the sky. 'Aren't they great?' he said. 'What a spectacle!'

'I'll bet you could never do that,' Lionel said from the depths of his armchair.

Dick sat up. 'Say that again?'

'I said: I'll bet you couldn't do that.'

Dick looked at him: 'How much?'

'Five quid.'

'You're on!'

Next morning Lionel had forgotten all about it. However, three days later he and Eileen were sitting in deckchairs in their garden enjoying a glass of wine under the blazing midsummer sun, when they heard the splutter of a small aircraft in the distance.

Lionel recalled: 'The sound increased. Then, over the trees at a height of three hundred feet, appeared a Tiger Moth with a familiar silhouette riding on top of the wing, strapped to a kind of zimmer frame. No prizes for guessing who it was up there. Fearless Fred himself! Dick flew straight over my garden, saw us sitting there and gave us a wave of triumph, like some Roman emperor of old.

'I waved back. But when the phone rang half an hour later, I refused to believe it was him. "That wasn't you," I said. "You're making it up!" I could hear him practically dancing with rage on the other end. "It was me!" he shouted. "It *was*!"

'Of course, I knew it was Dick and I was just winding him up. It was an amazing stunt. But even when he produced a photograph showing him strapped to the wing, I told him: "It's a fake!"

'He was livid, especially when I refused to pay him the five pounds! He never let me forget it. Every time we met after that, he'd stick out his palm and say: "C'mon, where's that fiver? Hand it over!" But I never did.'

Dick's mother didn't escape the 'flying experience' either and actually enjoyed being taken for a spin. At least she was with her darling boy. But on this 'wing walking' occasion he had brought her along to watch without telling her what he was planning to do.

'Wait here, Mum. I may be a little time,' he exhorted her. Bertha was left sitting in his Rolls Royce lighting up the first of numerous cigarettes. Meanwhile her son strode manfully off across the airfield, donned his flying kit in the small changing hut, emerged to be escorted to his blue and yellow Tiger Moth and clambered onto the upper wing to be strapped into the harness.

A face appeared at the car window. 'Look at Dick!' an enthusiastic onlooker shouted. 'Isn't he mad?'

Bertha stared out through the window as the Tiger Moth bumped over the grass. 'What's the bloody fool up to now?' was all she said . . . but she chain-smoked until her son was safely back on terra firma.

18. Familiar Faces

'Pardon'

MANDY

Back at the BBC the first show Ernest Maxim and Dick did together was a taste of things to come – and a huge challenge to both star and producer. It was thirty minutes of fast-moving sketches, with Dick playing *every one* of the characters, the only outsiders being back shots of people he was supposed to be talking to.

'We got through it with trick photography and a lot of imagination,' Ernest recalled. His own favourite sketch, which he wrote himself, was called *Grand Prix*. It featured the aged Lampwick lusting after Hettie, whose recourse to keep him at arm's length was to tell him she would only marry him if he won a vintage car race – at his own vintage age of eighty-five.

Undaunted, the old warrior gets hold of an open-top T-Ford and restores it until it's ready to race. 'Dick played all the other racing drivers – the smooth Italian, the young Swede and the rest.' But Lampwick knows he isn't going to be quick enough, so he doctors all the rival cars. One goes off the track with a flat tyre and another explodes when it overtakes him.

'We shot the sketch at Snetterton race track in Norfolk and that sequence, complete with split screen, was as spectacular as a real movie.' The show itself notched up a record seventeen million viewers.

Who wins? 'The old boy, of course. In the end Hettie runs into his arms and we had a lovely emotional finish.'

During one lunch break, Dick decided he wanted to have a spin round the track in one of the souped-up racers. Knowing his star as 'a bit of a daredevil', Ernest wasn't too happy. 'For God's sake, be careful, Dick,' he warned.

Today he recalls: 'Dick went tearing round that track like a madman, flat out round the bends while I was breaking out in a cold sweat because I honestly didn't think he would come back. When he finally brought her in, he climbed out and said nonchalantly: "This car should be able to go faster!"'

After all that, Ernest's own soft spot, like Dick's, was for Lampwick. 'We made him so lovable you never laughed against him, you laughed with him.

'We used to laugh so much together at rehearsals that I sometimes wonder how we ever got through them. I knew which buttons to press to make Dick chuckle, you see.

'For instance, my mother came from Leeds and I told him about a man who ran a corner shop there whose name was Zebediah Twine. Somehow Dick found that hysterical and insisted on inventing a character with that name – except that he could never get his tongue around it! You try saying it fast.

'He quite liked swapping jokes but not as much as anecdotes. One that had him falling about much later on was about a curry house that opened in Bradford. "They call it the Boycott. You still get the runs but they don't come so quickly!"'

Away from the spotlight, Ernest found Dick 'the most appreciative man I ever worked with'. In what sense? 'He appreciated what the writers, the cameramen and the producers did to make the show work. A lot of comedians like to feel that it's all coming from them and nobody else. Dick wasn't like that. He was always buying me little presents, despite my protests. An electric razor one day, or he'd stroll in with a tie and plant it on my desk for no reason.

'"It's the only way I can show my appreciation," he'd say.

'And I would retort: "The only way to show it is to trawl up the ratings!" And we did.'

Ernest had already achieved some remarkable successes in that direction, showing the Midas touch when it came to the pulse of public opinion. Notably among his credits would be *The Morecambe and Wise Show*, in which he doubled the ratings from thirteen million to more than twenty-eight million in six weeks. The secret, as he always said, was sensing what the public wanted – and not what the lords and masters at the Beeb or ITV *thought* they should want.

Despite the word among insiders in the business that Dick (unlike Morecambe and Wise) would not have other stars on his show, Ernest is adamant in that the only reason was that he would have overshadowed them with his huge roll-call of characters.

'Dick was so happy with the way we were working as a team that he didn't want to bring in anyone else. All the supporting people in the shows were excellent actors, each and every one of them. Which is why we used them whenever we could.' Indeed, the faces in the crowd became familiar to fireside viewers like old friends popping in for a cup of tea and a chat.

One of the most familiar faces on *The Dick Emery Show* belonged to Pat Coombs. A warm, friendly comedienne in her own right, 'Patty' as Dick called her, belonged to the old reliable school of acting – never late for rehearsals, always turning in a stalwart performance and no histrionics to upset the others.

Radio was Patty's true forte and she popped up regularly from the 50s to the 90s – though as often as not you wouldn't know it was her until the announcer read the credits at the end because the voices were so realistic. She went from radio to TV's popular *Beggar My Neighbour,* playing Reg Varney's wife, and later to a key role in *EastEnders* as downtrodden spinster Marge.

She and Dick set eyes on each other for the first time in the Lowestoft summer show in 1956. She had reached that particular high spot in her career after the first hint of a talent to amuse began as a child, when she found she could imitate her sister crying. Next step was to impersonate her teachers at college – one of whom had the sense to spot the potential in the cheeky young miss and encourage her to go to drama school.

'It was my first summer season – and Dick's umpteenth,' she recalled. 'He was an established entertainer – I was quite new to the business and a little scared. But he was wonderful to me, always encouraging and always with laughter.'

Eventually she would become a regular on *The Dick Emery Show*, appearing in scores of sketches between 1960 and the late 70s, when the series was drawing in millions of viewers.

'Dick was an absolute joy to work with. I was usually the next-door neighbour when he was dressed up as a woman who gossiped over the garden fence or came round to complain about something.'

'The Neighbour' was a perfect illustration of their love-hate screen relationship. 'The title became the easy way for people to identify the bitchy, ruthless, domineering woman who always comes off best – that's me,' Dick declared. 'Nasty, spiteful, envious, malicious, a truly bad neighbour. Oh, it was wonderful.'

The sketch ran like this (and note the names of the rabbits):

SCENE: *Two back gardens divided by a fence. The garden on the right is neatly kept, with a goldfish pond surrounded by stone gnomes, flowers along the fence and a small rabbit hutch.*

The other garden is a shambles, littered with rusty bicycle frames and overflowing dustbins. Ethel (Dick) emerges from the back door in a headscarf over ginger wig and curlers, bedroom slippers and a cigarette dangling from her mouth.

She leans over the fence where a large marrow is growing, produces a pair of scissors and snips the marrow off its stem. Win (Patty) appears, and Ethel hastily shoves the marrow under her pinafore.

ETHEL: Win! Hello, love. You're back a day early. Well I never. Did you have a nice time?

WIN: Hello, Ethel. Yes, wonderful. (*Her eyes travel down to the bulge under Ethel's pinny.*) Ooh, I say! Ethel, you haven't!

ETHEL: Haven't what, love?

WIN: After all this time – you haven't fallen?

ETHEL: (*looking down uncomfortably*) Oh no. I ate some home-made bread for breakfast and I think it's still rising.

WIN: Well, I mustn't stand here gossiping.

ETHEL: Well, I always think of you as almost part of my own family.

WIN: (*hanging washing*) So do I. Aren't we lucky? Never a cross word.

ETHEL: You know my motto: 'Do unto others . . .'

WIN: By the way, did you remember to feed my rabbits?

ETHEL: Er . . . well, not exactly.

Win moves to the hutch and looks inside.

WIN: (*horrified*) My gawd! They've gone. What happened?

ETHEL: You're never going to believe this . . .

WIN: Oooh! Oooh, you never ate Eric and Ernie! Oh, I don't know what my Wally'll say. He was so fond of those rabbits he was going to have them stuffed.

ETHEL: They were, dear. With sage and onion.

WIN: By the way, what happened to my Cox's Orange Pippin?

ETHEL: You're what—?

WIN: My apple tree. There's not a bit of fruit left on it.

ETHEL: Well, you did say I could have all the windfalls.

WIN: Yes, but I heard nothing on the news about a flaming hurricane.

And on it goes, with Win being outsmarted at every turn despite her protestations.

Patty was one of the clever ones who managed to take the best of Dick and leave the rest! She recalls: 'The truth is that we both valued our friendship more than anything, and Dick wanted me as a friend for life rather than just a one-night stand or a quick affair. I've always seen that as a wonderful compliment.

'I still treasure the time in 1978 when I was presented with the famous Big Red Book by Eamon Andrews for *This Is Your Life*. There was Dick speaking on the screen to me from Leeds, where he was in pantomime.

'He said: "Ever since we met, Patty, we have had tears running down our cheeks. It's a wonderful thing to have such laughter between two people as we have had." Wasn't that lovely?'

Pat, remembering the laughter, says simply: 'Now? The years pass, but I'll never forget him. Never.'

Nor will Joan Sims or Peter Elliott, two other stalwarts who did

Trojan service in the Emery camp. Blonde and bubbly, Joan was once described somewhat unkindly as 'overweight, a sweet woman and a good laugh'. Believe it or not, she didn't mind a bit! But if you knew her, you also knew that would be her reaction.

Joan and Dick had a lot in common, so much so that it was probably written in the stars that they would meet and she would become an integral part of the team. Like Dick, she was a bag of nerves when she started out in show business as 'a slim young woman with very little self-assurance. I was never sure about my looks and I was never confident about myself as a girl.' As someone wrote at the time: 'Behind the laughs is the story of a lonely child who flirted with failure' . . . Yet eventually, in true show-business tradition, she would win through.

The daughter of a stationmaster from Laindon, Essex, Joan was accepted into RADA at the fourth attempt and from then on hated all auditions and interviews. 'I just found them so inhibiting,' she confided to Dick one day.

'Me too, old love,' was Dick's response.

After cutting her teeth in repertory and West End musical reviews, Joan joined the Emery clan and became another familiar face in the series. She would go onto be part of a different 'surrogate family' – the *Carry On* crowd, no less, pitting her wits against the various advances of Kenneth Williams, Charles Hawtrey, Kenneth Connor, Jim Dale and, of course, becoming the regular object of Sid James's lascivious affections.

Consummate actress and comedienne that she was, Joan fitted into the Dick Emery team as if they had been waiting for her, and enjoyed several years as a 'regular' before joining the *Carry On* mob for yet more laughter.

All this time, Ernest Maxim kept a very close watch on everything and everyone. 'Dick wouldn't suffer fools gladly,' he recalled, 'and being the complete professional he couldn't stand inefficiency. But he didn't shout or rave, he wasn't that kind of person. He would close up. But I only had to look at him to sense his mood.'

As for his sense of humour: 'It was boyish, not filthy. I never heard him swear. The great thing about working with Dick was that he could always see the funny side in anything, even in somebody walking down the street towards us. He'd say: "Look at that chap! I'll bet he's brilliant at DIY . . . and that one, he probably spends every night in the pub . . . or that one, I'll bet he plays with a Meccanno set!" He could fantasize about everybody.

'Some days, I might say: "We need new characters, Dick. Have a look at the passers-by and see if you can find anything." And he always came up with someone.'

They soon had the logistics of the show down to a fine art. Ernest described the schedule: 'I would give the writers (John Warren and John Singer) the story outline for the sketches, and they went away and wrote the dialogue. They were great writers, I can tell you! And Dick knew it too. He always said: "You are only as good as your script," and gave credit to the writers for "making" the show.

'I used to look through the scripts and maybe think of a gag or two that might go in, then show the result to Dick in my office on a Monday morning. He might say: "Can I use this . . . or that . . . ?" And I'd be delighted because it meant he was giving everything to it.

'We did a half-hour show a week, thirteen shows a year. Starting with rehearsals on Monday afternoon, then working through every day until Friday. It was a tough schedule. The show itself was recorded on Saturday night in the BBC studio, with an audience. I never, ever, used canned laughter.

'On Saturday we'd finish tying up the loose ends at 6.00 p.m. The audience came in at 7.30 p.m., and I'd go out and do a warm-up for ten minutes – it's always great fun getting the folks keyed up for the star. At 8.00 p.m. we'd begin the show and we had to be out of there before 10.00 p.m. Otherwise it was overtime and the lights would go out!

'In all the years I worked with Dick we always finished on time – or early.'

Ernest knew that what went on behind the cameras was as vital as what went on in front. He took exceptional pains to keep his cast happy and the atmosphere light, and along with *The Dick Emery Show* applied this principle to his other entertainment blockbusters like Dave Allen, Charlie Drake, Les Dawson and Morecambe and Wise, all of them award winners at various festivals.

Ernest Maxim had been a major influence behind the scenes – and now Peter Elliott made an impact on both sides of the camera. Dick and

Peter had met briefly in the mid-50s on *Educating Archie,* when Peter visited friends in the studio. 'I liked Dick. I thought he had a great personality and we hit it off from the word go,' recalled Peter, who years later would become executive administrator in charge of Brinsworth House, the famous Residential Home for Retired Variety Artistes in Twickenham, Surrey, where such noted entertainers as Ben Warris and Charlie Chester spent their last days.

'In *Educating Archie* Dick did voices and a bit of "feeding". It was funny because he was straight man to a dummy!' Peter was part of a double act called Edmundson and Elliott, a comedy patter duo who toured the country halfway down the bill, making a fair to decent living out of clubs and seaside shows.

In 1966 Peter found himself in Cardiff, where he had been hired with his partner for the Christmas attraction of *Mother Goose,* with Dick in the title role – and, naturally, in drag. It was to be a lucrative sixteen-week run in the gravy-train days when pantomimes ran throughout the winter and kept the cast secure and solvent on the cold dark nights.

But – a small problem arose. A month before, Peter had been in a major car accident with Ben Warris and had broken his leg with eleven multiple fractures. Now, fresh out of hospital, he was hobbling around with his right leg encased in plaster up to the hip – hardly a portent for fun and games on the stage of the Grand Theatre. He needed the work, so how to disguise it?

It was not easy but Peter worked out a solution. He had a pair of trousers specially made with one leg larger than the other so that it would fit over the plaster cast. On the first day of rehearsals he arrived at the Stage Door swinging one huge gammy leg like Long John Silver without an apparent care in the world.

'We'd been booked in for sixteen weeks to be the broker's men. It was good money and I didn't want to lose it.

'Dick greeted me like an old friend and made no reference to the way I was walking or the size of my right leg. We did two days' rehearsal, with me swaying around trying to keep my balance – and still no comment. But finally the manager called me to one side.

'"Don't mind me asking, son – but why are you walking like that?" he asked. "Is there something wrong?"

178

'I came clean and when he heard he went ballistic! "Do you realize what would happen if you were knocked down in the show?" he shouted. "It would cost us a fortune. I'm sorry – but you'll have to go." So I was out.

'Dick heard about it. He went straight to the management. "Better get another Mother Goose," he told them. "If Peter goes, I go."

'Of course there was a terrific row. Finally Dick said: "Tell you what, I've got an idea. We'll make him the village idiot! He can wear a long smock and a hat with straw hanging out of it and he can have a staff to support him so he doesn't fall over . . ."

'It was a brilliant idea. Dick rewrote the scenes himself. The only thing was that there had to be a blackout every time I entered, with the stage plunged into darkness.

'All you could hear was *clump! clump! clump!* Then someone would whisper: *"He's here!"* and the lights would go up and Dick would say: "Hello, look who it is: the village idiot!" and we'd carry on with the scene. When I'd finished, the lights went out again and all you'd hear was *clump! clump! clump!* as I limped off.'

But why the blackout? 'Because we might have disabled people in the audience, and they'd think I was taking the mickey out of them. At least they didn't put me in a wheelbarrow . . .'

Dick actually disliked 'doing panto' intensely, though only those closest to him knew it. The reason: 'In those days he wasn't over fond of children,' says Peter. 'He liked them in small doses, but not in huge dollops! I remember one matinee we were doing *Mother Goose* and Dick came walking through the corridor backstage in a crinoline dress and a huge hat with a feather in it. He said to me: "What a terrible row's going on out there this afternoon. I've never heard so much noise before a show. What's going on?"

'I told him: "Oh, they've got eight hundred children in from local orphanages."

'Dick stared at me. "What!" he exclaimed. "Eight *hundred. Eight hundred bloody kids!* Fancy bringing kids to a pantomime." Then he looked at me, realized what he'd said, and we both fell about laughing.

'When we finally stopped laughing, I stared at him and said, deadpan: "You're right. Anybody would think we're doing all this for children!" Wonderful!'

That was Dick. He could be as funny when he didn't mean to be as when he was being paid for it.

Following sixteen weeks of pantomime, Peter was taken onto the team as a 'feed', trying to keep his face immobile as the straight man in lightning sketches which were over so fast that if you blinked, you'd miss them. That summer, in seaside shows from Brighton to Skegness, the sketches grew longer – mainly because the pair were by now ad-libbing with the script thrown out of the window.

In one favourite sketch, Peter would be sitting in a deckchair on the beach and old Lampwick would come shuffling up. 'We had a two-minute synopsis, but then we just went off in all directions,' Peter recalled. 'We could ad-lib for up to twenty minutes. I know it sounds like a dangerous game to play, but it worked terribly well – and audiences loved it.'

At the end of the season, Peter was invited to join *The Dick Emery Show* on TV and became the interviewer in countless sketches, armed with a microphone, approaching Dick in all his various guises.

It was in one of these early 'confrontations' with perhaps the most familiar face of them all, Mandy, that the country first heard: 'Ooh, you are awful – but I like you!'

INTERVIEWER: Now here comes a charming young lady.

MANDY: Hello—

INTERVIEWER: Tell me, do you have good neighbours?

MANDY: Well, I live in a hostel for young ladies. The girls are ever so friendly, but we're having trouble with the landlord.

INTERVIEWER: Really, what about?

MANDY: He objects to us having pin-ups on the wall.

INTERVIEWER: So are you girls going to give in and take them down for him?

MANDY: Pardon?

INTERVIEWER: Or are you going to hang onto yours and stop him tearing them off?

MANDY: Ooh, you are awful – but I like you!

Thwack!

And it was Peter who got the first thump from the outrageous blonde coquette.

19. Top Speed

'Fantastic, that's what it is. Fantastic!'

TON-UP BOY

Dick made no secret of his love of speed and as success followed success from 1964 onwards, his career went into overdrive. He continued the pattern of seaside shows in the summer, pantomime in the winter, and TV and radio in between. As his popularity grew the whole world seemed to be clamouring for his services. There was always a fête or shop to open, a beauty contest to judge or a hospital to visit. There was also the lucrative world of advertising, and many of his characters could be seen or heard singing the praises of anything from washing machines to custard powder on TV and radio.

This fast lifestyle suited Dick very well as it didn't give him time to dwell on his personal problems, but in February 1964 he did find time to marry Victoria, having eventually managed to convince Iris that he was not going back. When she realized he had a new home and another baby she had to accept it, however reluctantly, although she never stopped loving him. This added to Dick's guilt, and the guiltier he felt the harder he worked. If he had any free time, he knew how to distract himself. He took to the road in a variety of 'metal steeds' of increasing power and performance as his financial position improved. He changed cars and motorbikes the way other men change their shirts and the early 'old bangers', including a vintage Bentley, had given way to more modern vehicles.

Pride of place went to an E-Type Jaguar and then, of course, there was the inevitable Rolls Royce, the essential status symbol to reflect his fame and fortune.

Dick never did anything by halves. Right or wrong he threw himself into everything he did with all his might, and wasn't afraid to explain himself. In his own words:

The fact is that to compensate for being small, I need to surround myself with as large and powerful a machine as possible. The bigger they are, the more I love 'em. And if they're bristling with chrome and gadgets, so much the better.

The first sight of the sophisticated modern bikes makes my jaw drop in wonderment. Unless one is a staid old puss, one cannot help but be agog at the brilliant designs.

I remember biking back in the 30s and the great names blaring out from the pages of the bike magazines. Those were the days when Nortons were in the forefront. You were somebody if you owned a Norton and in the money too. It would cost anything between ninety and a hundred pounds. As for the Brough Superior – if you owned one of those you were in the Rolls Royce class.

One of my first bikes was an old heap called a DOT, which I bought for ten shillings. The engine was 100cc and in a very rough condition. I removed the cylinder head and piston and when they were repaired I had the exquisite joy of putting it all together again.

The following was written a few years later but on the same theme:

I own a machine which is the largest in its range: a BMW RT1000 – a splendid beast with practically everything on it bar the kitchen sink, including an electric clock! She behaves beautifully. There is a tremendous satisfaction to see a whole line of cars up ahead and to sidle up on the outside just as the lights turn green. Then – away! Counting the gears, second, third, fourth, then fifth. What joy.

Whatever pressures are weighing on me, I can always escape and lose myself in precision driving at speed. It is my one unfailing safety valve. After a few hours of total concentration I'm ready to come back and face the world.

In 1965 Dick made another attempt to break into films. He had a supporting role in *The Big Job*, a crime comedy with Sid James and Joan Sims. *Intelligence Men*, *The Wrong Box*, *The Knack* and *Baby Love* followed. He was still playing supporting roles and he wanted to be the star, but that honour was confined to TV and live shows, where the public made it clear they liked him best.

186

At home, on the rare occasions that he was there, he tried hard to play happy families with Victoria, but as usual the endless separations due to his work and her commitment to the boutique caused them to quarrel. On one of their few evenings out together Dick and Victoria joined Max Bygraves and his wife Blossom to attend the first night of a play in Leatherhead, Surrey.

The play was *The Match Girls*, and one of the actresses was a high-stepping blonde beauty who immediately caught Dick's eye. He studied the programme. Her name was Josephine Blake. Dick was hooked again and found out her phone number. 'No harm in a little chat,' he tried to fool himself. But by the following February, 1966, when Victoria presented him with their second child, his only daughter, Eliza, what should have been a joyous occasion was sadly marred by growing signs of discontent.

Once again Dick tried to lose himself in work.

In pantomime he invariably played the dame, and always with a wicked twinkle in his eyes. He started to collect a fabulous wardrobe of lavish frocks and ingenious props, including a pair of large dangling earrings wired to a hidden battery that flashed on at appropriate moments.

'Playing the dame is exhausting,' Dick confided. 'With two shows a day and up to thirty-six costume changes, it's one mad rush from the moment I arrive at the theatre.'

He did his own make-up, took personal care of his many wigs and struggled in and out of tights, high-heeled shoes, crinoline dresses and long frilly knickers, all without the aid of a dresser. There was no backstage help for Dick. He did it his way – extremely methodical and careful, putting away his props and his make-up so that everything was close to hand when he needed it in a hurry.

There was one dramatic backstage incident that Dick would never forget. It occurred when he was starring (as Baron Hardup) in *Cinderella* at Streatham in South London, when the theatre nearly burned down.

The cast included Joe Brown as Buttons, John Inman as one of the ugly sisters with Peter Elliott playing the Baron's effusive secretary.

Peter takes up the story: 'It was a great cast and a great show. However, backstage all was not as it seemed! There were seven fellers who ran everything and they were all brothers. We called them the

Magnificent Seven. The only problem was that they were as thick as two short planks!

'We had a very gay guy looking after the clothes – Michael. We called him the Wardrobe Mistress. One afternoon as we arrived for the matinee, we heard him screaming: *"The wardrobe's alight! The wardrobe's alight!"* The wardrobe was in fact a large room packed with all the clothes for the show.

'Michael had done something to a washing machine, there'd been a short-circuit and now there were flames leaping out everywhere! There was pandemonium and Dick shouted: "Tell the stage door keeper to get the fire brigade!" I raced over and found the stage door keeper, one of the seven brothers, reading a newspaper.

'"Get the fire brigade, quick!" I said. "The wardrobe's on fire!" "Oh, right," he said.

'I rushed back and found Dick throwing jugs of water on the blaze. After a few minutes he said: "Where's the bloody fire brigade?" I rushed back and the guy's got the phone book out and is thumbing through it.

'"Excuse *me!*" I said. "But what exactly are you doing?"

'He said: "You told me to ring the fire brigade. Is it under 'F' or 'B'?"

'"No one's going to believe this," I said. "Haven't you ever heard of 999?"

'"Oh yeah," he replied. "But that's only for an emergency."

'I shouted: "What do you think this is! The bloody theatre's alight!"

'"Oh, yeah, I suppose it is," he said. By which time I'd snatched the phone from him and dialled 999 myself."'

The fire brigade saved the theatre – and it gave Dick and Peter a story to dine out on for years to come.

With pantomime over for another year, Dick concentrated on improving and expanding his characters once more. He could be quite acerbic when he wanted, especially when discussing his old friend the Vicar. Speaking bluntly about real television vicars he said: 'To me, they seem to be a breed apart, totally divorced from reality.

'I've watched them intoning the same old pious platitudes in religious broadcasts and nightly epilogues in voices which must surely be reserved for their TV appearances. Imagine them asking someone to pass the marmalade or scolding the cat in those precious measured tones!'

Dick's own religious convictions had nothing to do with it, though it seems he was more agnostic than atheist. This was personal, a dislike of what he saw as humbug and cant, neither of which he could stand. 'I hope I don't give the impression that I'm denigrating the Christian religion in my Vicar,' he said, and he meant it. 'Far from it. What I try to bring out in the character is the patent insincerity that I feel underlies many of its ministers. They're becoming more like show-business performers in their attempts to increase their following.'

As usual Dick waded straight in. With his brutally honest approach and eye for detail, he didn't miss a trick and he explained: 'The protruding front teeth of my Vicar immediately make him a comic character. But I think they also help him achieve that sanctimonious, butter-wouldn't-melt-in-my-mouth look. Having inadvertently disclosed his true nature while answering the interviewer's question, he has to compose his features around those teeth to resume his usual expression of bland piety!'

INTERVIEWER: Excuse me, Vicar.

VICAR: Yes, my son?

INTERVIEWER: As a man of the Church, I am sure you have the interests of the community very much at heart.

VICAR: Oh, yes indeed. For instance, on behalf of my flock I have been keeping a critical eye on some of the scandalous strip clubs in the neighbourhood.

INTERVIEWER: And what are your conclusions?

VICAR: Well, for my money you can't beat Miss Lulu and her trained pythons at the Girlies Galore.

And of course there was Mandy. The overdressed flirtatious blonde, with whom Dick is instantly associated through half a century and into posterity, who grew out of his Gang Show 'Vera Thin'.

But to tell the truth, Dick didn't like Mandy. He was not totally enamoured with the feminine side of his professional persona. Those who watched him become Mandy, Hettie or other female characters, noted that when wearing drag he went to great lengths to appear butch rather than bitch.

Producer and long-standing friend Harold Snoad pointed out: 'Dick would hitch up his skirts and walk around in an extremely ungainly fashion, while using a deep Cockney accent and some fairly ripe language!

'He seemed desperately anxious that no member of the public should think that he in any way enjoyed dressing up as a woman. When we were filming, Dick spent his time between shots scanning the crowd to ensure nobody managed to take a photo without him knowing. He was perfectly prepared to pose – but not if he wasn't ready for it. Many was the time that I'd be talking to him, when he'd spot a movement in the crowd and shift his feet so that I was between him and the snapper.'

Dick confirmed it: 'Dare I admit that I have no great love for the female characters I portray? I never present a "nice" woman, perhaps because deep inside I resent the suggestion that I am a female impersonator.

'Of all my characters, Mandy is actually the least real to me personally. Everything about her seems larger than life. Whereas the others are genuine people, she remains a theatrical figure and I have to admit that she's rather difficult to live with because wherever I go someone is always ready to deliver her punchline!'

Dick denied having purposefully created Mandy, she just seemed to grow. He often complained about her as if she were nothing to do with him.

'Despite my feelings about her, she seems to have achieved an identity of her own. Which reminds me,' Dick added, 'she once dislocated the poor interviewer's shoulder with an over-enthusiastic punch! It just goes to show how dangerous it is to tangle with blondes . . .'

The Interviewer was certainly long-suffering:

INTERVIEWER: What a charming young lady . . .

MANDY: Thank you.

INTERVIEWER: Tell me, do you believe in extra-sensory perception?

MANDY: Oh yes, I do. I'm rather psychic myself.

INTERVIEWER: Can you give me an example?

MANDY: Well, the very first time I met my boyfriend, I knew instinctively that we were completely compatible.

INTERVIEWER: You mean, you sensed there was something between you?

MANDY: Pardon?

INTERVIEWER: You immediately felt his vibrations?

MANDY: Ooh, you are awful – but I like you!

Whack!

When not dreaming up a new character, rehearsing for TV or rushing up and down the country to perform in a theatre show, Dick put a good deal of his energy and spare time into helping children in deprived areas, or the sick and elderly. He seemed to need to repay society for his good fortune and increasing wealth.

Unheralded and unsung, he visited countless children's homes and hospitals and always managed to get a smile out of his youthful audience.

The only condition he made was: 'No publicity.' Sometimes word got out and there would be a TV camera or a photographer lurking at the entrance. But more often than not Dick stayed anonymous, even paying out of his own pocket for a child to have an operation privately when he heard that the waiting list was too long on the National Health Service.

Other times, a kid longing for a bike would find a gleaming new machine waiting for him at the hospital gates when he was discharged to go home. It happened more than once, though the public never knew about it.

Dick continued to rush headlong into his life and seemed to thrive on it, but deep down it must have taken its toll, as such pressure invariably does. On the surface everything looked wonderful. The public loved him. The producers loved him. The children he visited loved him. But he judged himself more harshly and couldn't love himself. Finding his home life unsatisfactory, he refused to listen to his conscience and became more and more dependent on his growing relationship with Josephine, as he hankered after new delights.

In 1967 Victoria couldn't take any more. She was strong enough to withstand the agonizing indecision in which Dick wallowed. She sued him for a divorce, naming Josephine Blake as the 'Intervener'. The divorce became absolute in 1968. Although left with two very young children and a business to run, Victoria dried her tears and got on with her life in peace.

Not so Dick as he agonized over what he had done, wept buckets, and was tormented by his demons again. His mother, of course, was delighted and expected her son to return 'home'. Instead, he went back to Iris, thinking he could rekindle their relationship.

Once again, work came to the rescue when Dick was asked to pioneer the BBC's new colour techniques. For the first time he was seen in colour on BBC2. It was a great hit and repeated on BBC1 the next year. From then on *The Dick Emery Show* was in the top TAM's rating lists.

Life with Iris still didn't work, and in yet more floods of tears Dick left her and set up home with Josephine in a flat in London. She was working at the Prince of Wales Theatre as one of the principals in the smash show *Sweet Charity*. Dick was dazzled by her strength and beauty, and a quality he interpreted as 'Look, but don't touch'. It made him desperate to touch! Two years after their meeting, Josephine and Dick were married in November 1969 and moved into a beautiful house on an exclusive estate in Weybridge, Surrey.

At last Dick believed he had everything he had longed for. A gorgeous, head-turning wife, a luxury home, a successful career and no money worries. Bertha still insisted on being telephoned every day, and on the rare occasions he failed to get in touch with her for two or three days he would get the 'Thank God, I thought you were dead!' treatment sobbed down the line.

But now even Bertha couldn't spoil his euphoria.

20. Non-Stop

'My money's on Lulu'

THE VICAR

Getting his business affairs in order was now a priority for Dick, as the paperwork involved in administrating *being* 'Dick Emery' was piling up. He acquired a small office in Baker Street, opposite those famous consulting rooms of Mr Sherlock Holmes at 221b.

Fan letters were stacked in one corner and messages piled up to be answered: in short, the place was chaotic. It was time to find a secretary.

'I started asking around and soon realized that it was going to be impossible to find the right person,' he recalled. 'I was desperate. The person would have to be knowledgeable about show business without wanting to get into it themselves, and be on call twenty-four hours a day.

'The other essentials included having a fantastic sense of humour and an iron reserve to cope with all the last-minute panics, as well as being good-looking and smart enough to cope with me – and my mum!' For, as always, the forbidding shadow of Bertha still loomed large in the background.

The answer was Margaret Thomas. An attractive, vivacious woman in her forties, Margaret's background had been running her own successful tobacconist's shop in Charing Cross Road, then helping her husband with his musical-instrument business, looking after the clerical side and the accounts.

Dick hired her on the spot because he thought she had a kind face – or at least that's what he told her at their first meeting round the corner from her flat in Marylebone. She had been woken early in the morning and summoned to the studio where her future boss was making a commercial.

'I remember being woken up very early, much to my annoyance as I had had a late night,' Margaret recalls with a smile, looking back on the phone call that changed her life. 'The studio was practically next door, so it wasn't far to walk. It was managed by a friend of mine, Pat.

'"Come over right away!" Pat said. The request wasn't unusual, as I was always getting calls when small items that I could supply were needed in a hurry.

'I can still see her face when I walked into her office above the studio ten minutes later. "You might have put a comb through your hair," she said. "You look as if you've just got out of bed!"

'"I have," I told her. "Why the panic?"

'"Dick Emery's here and he wants to talk to you."

'Why me? I wasn't particularly impressed as I'd met a lot of showbiz people, and always found them amusing." Then Dick came upstairs, looking exceedingly smart in a dark suit. He took one look at me and said simply: "Hello, darling. I'm looking for a secretary and I think you'll do. Would you like to come and work for me?"

'I blinked back at him. "I don't need a job – besides, you don't know anything about me!" I managed to stammer out.

'Dick said: "That's all right. Pat's told me all I need to know. You sound just right. I need looking after, my affairs are in a mess and you've got a kind face! Think it over and I'll call you at 10.00 a.m. tomorrow."

'With that he was gone. I forgot all about it – but next morning, prompt at ten, the phone rang and there he was on the other end of it. The upshot was that I went round to his tiny office in Baker Street to see what was in store if I took the job on. Saying it was a mess was the understatement of the year. But Dick looked so lost, how could I say no?'

So from 1969, Margaret stayed with Dick for the next fourteen years, and her initial employment as a secretary grew into a friendship that would last the rest of his life. She became his tower of strength, as personal assistant, accountant, advisor and best friend.

'It started with a complete reorganization of the office, then getting all his business affairs in order. It took weeks, but it was worth it. And suddenly I was a permanent fixture!' Margaret remembers those times with nostalgia.

'Our years together were exciting, sometimes traumatic, always hectic.

They were a challenge I accepted gladly. We became the best of friends and at times the best of enemies, when I knew he was heading for trouble but wouldn't listen!'

Dick grew to rely on her like a lifeline to an underwater diver. He would tell her: 'Margaret, if I ring you from Australia and ask you to go to Scotland on a bicycle, buy a ham sandwich and bring it to me yesterday – I know you'll do it!' And she probably would have.

Now that his paperwork was in hand, Dick felt more secure. He took off in all directions, along with his career. During 1969 came the first of twenty-one tours of Ireland, taking his show from Belfast to Dublin to Shannon and down south to Cork. 'And the best Guinness in the world,' he declared, with which the locals agreed.

The following year he cut his first album, an LP for Marble Arch Records produced by veteran bandleader Cyril Stapleton. It was called *Dick Emery Sings* and at last those mellifluous tones were recorded for posterity. Side one featured romantic ballads like 'If You Love Her', 'Wait for Me', 'Mine', My Own True Love', 'The Bells of St Mary's' and 'Love Will Find a Way'. Side two was in similar candlelight vein with 'Anyone Can Move a Mountain', 'The Girl Next Door', 'If Ever I Would Leave You', 'This is My Song' and 'Day After Day'.

If he wasn't quite in the Sinatra bracket, Dick still had a pleasant surprise during his first trek across Australia in concert with Judith Durham (of *The Seekers* fame) with a phone call out of the blue from Margaret back in London.

'You won't believe this, Dick. Your song "If You Love Her" has been released as a single and it's in the Top Twenty!'

Dick nearly dropped off his chair. 'Amazing!' he shouted. And, indeed, it was amazing. There had been no publicity and no promotion for the song whatsoever. On the strength of his voice alone, Dick had made it into the charts. Alas, because of his tour Down Under he never did get to sing on *Top of the Pops*, which surely would have been a feat to cherish for ever!

In 1970, Dick came home to star at the London Palladium with a supporting bill that included Russ Conway, Pete Murray, Roger Whittaker and Peter Noon with Herman's Hermits. This led to another milestone – king of the impresarios Bernard Delfont invited him to compere the Royal Variety Performance. Despite a last-minute attack of nerves, Dick 'lost' himself in his characters and they didn't let him down. The audience and the critics loved him. The boy from Balham shook hands with the Queen and he had not become too blasé to be excited.

On the evening of Saturday 29 August 1970, Dick was the castaway on *Desert Island Discs*. When asked by the show's creator Roy Plomley if he would mind being a castaway Dick's response was:

'No, I'm a bit of a loner. I can enjoy life being alone. I can organize myself better when I'm alone – with all due respect to my dear wife Josephine, who's possibly listening! Little Dicky is a good organizer.' He must have forgotten the lonely nights in hotel rooms when he couldn't bear his own company! But his choice of eight records took him from his early days of longing to be an opera singer through his romantic years, ending with comedy. 'They are almost identical to the happenings in my childhood and adult life,' he declared. The songs were: 'M'Appari Tutt'Amor', sung by Dick's hero Enrico Caruso, from the opera Marta; 'Shepherd Fennel's Dance', played by the New Symphony Orchestra; 'Love Was Young' sung by Robert Goulet; 'And I Love Her' by The Beatles; 'It Was a Very Good Year' by Frank Sinatra; 'You Don't Have to be Jewish' from the *Reading of the Will* by Jack Gilford and Lou Jacobi; an aria from Tosca sung by Benjamin Gigli; and 'That's All', a set of impressions of Bogart, Cagney and other Hollywood greats by Sammy Davis Jnr.

'I want to be able to say when I'm a very old gentleman and standing on the beach of this little island somewhere looking out to sea: *"Well, Dick boy, you had a go! It either worked or it didn't, but at least you had a go!"*'

As far as his marriage was concerned Dick felt he'd learned his lessons and was determined to keep Josephine happy. He was well aware of the sacrifice she had made – she had given up her career to become Mrs Dick Emery and share as much of his life as he could give to her. Together they went to parties, charity functions and Variety Club dinners. Josephine was even given small parts in his TV shows so she could at least keep one toe in the business.

Once he bought her a birthday present of an E-Type Jaguar, leading her to the front door with her eyes tight shut, before flinging the door open to reveal the car gift-wrapped in coloured plastic sheeting, complete with huge red bows. When he wanted to make an impression, Dick never did things by halves!

Now he indulged himself with another passion – boats. First off, he bought a thirty-foot Broom Seamaster, which he had fitted out to his exact specifications before delivery to a mooring spot on the Thames. After learning the ropes (and losing one when he threw it to the lock keeper to fasten, forgetting to tie the other end to his boat), Dick sold it in 1974, trading it in for a larger model more suitable, he felt, for sea-going.

'I'm going to conquer the waves,' he announced to a dubious but willing Josephine. He hired a skipper to help them make the maiden voyage from Norfolk to Torquay, so that he could learn how to handle the craft at sea. Unfortunately a squall blew up somewhere south of Canvey Island, and after lurching around the deck and hearing the crash of plates and glasses from the cabin, Dick decided to run for shelter.

They finally made it to Ramsgate. A wobbly Dick helped a green Josephine out of the bunk where she had spent most of the trip, and stepped onto dry land. They hired a car for the rest of the journey.

If fact, every time Dick took to the water it seemed to end with a dash to the nearest port as the wind howled around him and waves lashed the deck. One deceptively calm summer's day he persuaded himself to make a gentle sortie from Poole to nearby Bournemouth, where he had a rehearsal for a forthcoming show.

Dick dropped anchor in the harbour and went ashore in a dinghy. When the rehearsal was over he strolled back to the jetty in the sunshine – but the boat had gone. As he stared around in bewilderment, a woman approached.

'Are you looking for your boat, love?'

'Yes I am,' said Dick.

'Well, it's over there!' The woman pointed to a tiny dot on the horizon. 'I watched it drift out.'

Dick had failed to secure the anchor properly. It took him five hours to retrieve his modern-day *Marie Celeste*. Shortly after that incident, Dick decided he preferred to be a landlubber. So he sold the Broom Seamaster and contented himself with a Jupiter speedboat.

Dick was enjoying the fruits of success. Having spent so many years counting pennies, he was able to treasure the luxuries he could now afford. At home in Weybridge he would spend hours walking around his garden 'counting my blessings'. He had spent a lot on his home. He employed two gardeners, and the estate was landscaped with magnificent trees and flowering shrubs, immaculate lawns and flower beds ablaze with colour, particularly the roses which were Dick's favourites.

He paid a vast amount to create a swimming pool on the patio, with a sunroom, sauna and a gymnasium next to it. Inside he turned the interior of the house into a showcase straight out of *Homes and Gardens*. Including the most luxurious kitchen he could find!

In 1972, Dick fulfilled his ambition to star in a full-length feature film, a vehicle hand-crafted for him and entitled *Ooh, You Are Awful!* What else could it possibly have been named?

British Lion and Quintain Productions backed it, the enterprising Cliff Owen directed it and the tried-and-tested team of Warren and Singer wrote the screenplay. A cast of Britain's finest was brought in as back-up, led by Ronald Fraser, Derren Nesbitt, William Franklin and Pat Coombs.

The story revolved around the 'King of the Con Men', a Cockney confidence trickster named Charlie Tully, played by Dick. Charlie pulls off an unlikely scam against a wealthy Italian nobleman by 'arranging' a marriage between his son and Princess Anne, no less. The fee is half a millon pounds and when he finds he's been duped, the gullible signore calls on his pals in the Mafia to collect the half million – and dispose of the fraudster.

Charlie's sidekick (Ronnie Fraser) has safely stashed the loot in a Swiss bank. But the problem is that he meets an early demise. Charlie is left to track the money down himself. His job in piecing the numbers together as best he can is made much easier when he realizes his erstwhile partner in crime has tattooed the numerals that make up the account number on the buttocks of four gorgeous girls!

Cue the likes of Mandy, Lampwick, Hettie and a variety of familiar faces to make their appearance, as Charlie tracks down the comely quartet and finds various dubious ways of photographing the tattoos. In all Dick appeared as eight other characters. For ninety-seven minutes the farcical fun unfolds as the 'Con King' miraculously evades being bumped off while all around him the body count mounts up. In the end, of course, it all turns out fine with a clever and ridiculously funny final twist.

The film was well received, and still gets an occasional airing on TV. In America it was retitled *Get Charlie Tully* and did reasonable business, with one critic summing up the general view: 'Amusing star vehicle with plenty of room for impersonations and outrageous jokes'. Possibly on the strength of that, in 1976 Dick was asked to co-star with Mickey Rooney in a film made in Canada called *Find the Lady*. It was a crime spoof but Dick didn't think it was very good, and was relieved that it was never shown in Britain.

But it was a genuine thrill for him to meet and work with the legendary pint-sized star Mickey Rooney. At 5 feet 3 inches, he was even smaller than Dick, and they found they had a lot in common. Mickey, five years younger than Dick, regaled him with the story of how, as a child star spoiled and cosseted in the MGM stable, he was taken every Friday night into the office of the legendary Irving Thalberg, who ran the studios, and measured against the wall to see if he had grown during the week. 'They were worried sick that I'd grow too fast,' he recalled. 'I'm told the marks are still there to this day.'

'Well, that's a kind of immortality!' was all Dick could find to say, adding: 'They haven't found a wall for me – yet!'

This was Dick's last attempt to conquer the big screen, but he continued to be a workaholic. We often laughed about it together as he insisted on a doing almost any DIY job around the house. He had to 'have a go'. Putting up wall lights, towel rails and bathroom fittings came to him like a second vocation, and as a handyman he managed to turn potentially boring jobs into an entertainment, with a running commentary and plenty of repartee for anyone who assisted him. Generally his work was still in place the next day! We found that we shared the same game for getting through mundane jobs. We just imagined we were on a film set and placed our cameras at strategic points: we 'acted' peeling potatoes, cleaning the loo or whatever job it might be. It was strange to think that in our separate lives we had both been playing the 'game'.

'How about a cup of tea and a sit-down?' I would suggest hopefully. 'Not yet,' was the invariable answer. 'Just let me finish this shelf . . . cupboard . . . book case . . .' and on he would go.

He certainly didn't have time to stop in 1972. He was weighed down with the responsibility of his TV show and all the people dependent on it, and in his private life with an ever-growing list of people to support, he felt swamped. The pain of Bertha's rheumatoid arthritis sapped her valiant fighting spirit and she had to be cared for by nurses, day and night. Dick phoned her every day and visited frequently. He persuaded Margaret to stand in for him when he was overseas. Eventually Bertha had to be moved to a nursing home in Bournemouth, where she died in 1976 at the age of ninety-four. Dick was devastated. Despite the possessive stranglehold she had had on him for the whole of his life, his new-found freedom could never make up for his loss.

Losing touch with his children was another terror that haunted Dick. He wanted to be a good father but didn't have much experience to call on, and being divorced from their mothers didn't help. But he saw and financed them as much as he could, taking a keen interest in all they did, even if sometimes it was from the other side of the world.

Dick's punishing schedule started to take its toll. Although he looked fit – he worked out with weights every day – his body couldn't keep up with the stresses of his lifestyle. The first sign was that year, 1972. Dick was starring in his summer show at Southampton, when in his dressing room he suddenly doubled up with the most terrible pains. 'It was all over – chest, stomach, everywhere.' Margaret was with him. She put an urgent call through to his doctor, who drove straight down from London, gave Dick a brief examination and immediately decided he should to go to hospital – in Paddington. Josephine came to the rescue with a dramatic drive up the A3, breaking the speed limit, with Dick slumped in the back groaning in pain and the doctor following close behind. Thick fog turned the journey into a nightmare, but Josephine made it in record time and headed straight for St Mary's Hospital in Paddington, where the doctor had already phoned ahead to prepare them for Dick's arrival.

He was admitted to the Lindo Wing, where he underwent an emergency examination. The result was not good. He had gallstones, and then the frightening realization that his heart was in a bad state – so bad that an operation for the removal of the stones could not be carried out.

The doctor did not mince his words. 'You've had a heart attack,' he told his fretting patient bluntly. 'We're keeping you in.'

Dick was distraught. He was letting his public down. In Southampton the shows were cancelled and the money returned. But for once, he felt so ill that he succumbed to the inevitable and stayed in bed.

'The irony was that this whole drama happened at the same time that I was awarded a Silver Heart by the Variety Club as BBC Personality of the Year,' he said with a wry shrug. 'I watched the presentation on TV chewing the sheets in frustration as Josephine stepped up to collect the trophy on my behalf! I don't mind telling you that I broke down in tears.'

Dick's own words reflect his state of mind, writing about himself, but in the third person:

He'd had a good life, the latter part that is. His success started in middle age. Money came his way and he was able to buy the things he's always longed for, mainly cars and a fine house in its own grounds. And prestige. In fact money made it possible for him to indulge in most of the things that had been denied him in his youth.

But (there is always a 'but') to gain all these things he had to work, and work damned hard! When success finally came he was precipitated into a mad world, rushing from one place to another. He never stayed in one town or city for more than three months at a time. If that.

He wondered if it was all worthwhile. But he did not know how to stop.

And he didn't stop. Ignoring the evidence of the electrocardiogram, he discharged himself from hospital and carried on as usual.

21. Going Global

'I've got me finger in a lot of pies'

BOVER BOY

Dick was very well aware of the vital role played by his 'Interviewer', or straight man. The interviews had to be played for real, as Peter Elliott remembers: 'You had to get it into your mind that you really were interviewing a vicar or a biker or this awful woman. We modelled it on real TV interviews, although with nobody special, and we were always aware of how important it was to get it right. The straight man is no good without the comic and vice versa.'

Now Dick wanted a change of management and invited Peter to take over from Michael Sullivan. John Quale stepped into Peter's straight man shoes.

Peter was delighted to become Dick's personal manager – although he may have taken on more than he expected.

'Dick was very demanding. Sometimes he'd ring me twelve times a day – usually about little niggly things. But I kept him laughing and we stayed the best of friends – though sometimes I have to tell you it was a bit of a strain.

'Like the night he phoned me in the early hours, soon after I'd moved into a new house in Gerrard's Cross. It was winter, brass-monkey temperature, freezing cold and four o'clock in the morning. I'd got very little furniture, the house was a hollow echoing shell and the phone rang.

'Instinctively I knew it was Dick. He was doing a pantomime in Leeds, which he didn't want to do – but he owed a bit of money to the taxman so he had to go through with it ("it" being *Dick Whittington*) and because he was there under sufferance he was forever on the phone. He didn't like his dressing room, he didn't like the theatre and he didn't like Leeds!

'There's not actually a lot you can do in those circumstances, when you're in London and he's in Leeds. "The dressing room needs painting," Dick complained. So I got onto the manager. "Mr Emery's dressing room needs painting," I told him. "No, it doesn't", he replied. So what can you do?

'Now it's 4.00 a.m. and the only phone is downstairs. I was in bed and it started to ring and wouldn't stop. Finally, I gave in, stumbling down the stairs with no carpets and only nails sticking out, so I wasn't in the best of moods.

'"Oh," said Dick's voice. "I haven't woken you up, have I?"

'"Oh no," I assured him. "I'm always wandering about the house at four o'clock in the morning in the freezing cold."

'"Well," he said. "I've been pacing this hotel room all night, worried to death. I thought you should know—"

'"What's the problem?" I asked wearily.

'"We had this dress rehearsal tonight. It was chaos, absolute chaos, and the fairy dell hasn't arrived."

'"What—?"

'"The fairy dell hasn't arrived," he repeated firmly.

'There was a long pause while I thought about it. Finally I said: "Dick, how old are you?"

'He replied: "Er . . . sixty-four."

'"And you still believe in f***cking fairies?" I said and slammed the phone down. That's my job down the drain, I thought.

'Five minutes later, it rang again. I picked it up and I could hear his laughter. "That's very funny," he said. "It's brought it all back to reality. Thanks, mate!"'

Which says it all for the love-hate relationship between artists and their managers, doesn't it?

Having achieved a good working relationship, with laughter to sort out their difficulties, Peter felt confident enough to tell Dick that he should broaden his horizons. So in 1975 Peter negotiated a tour of Australia, where Dick's British TV series had been making big waves in the popularity charts. To his surprise and pleasure, Dick found he had already amassed a huge following. The Australians loved him. First stop was the Sydney Opera House, no less, and Peter remembers the hilarious opening night as if it were yesterday: 'Dick had a personal tailor named Giuseppe, in Shepherd's Bush in West London, close to the BBC studios. He made up all Dick's suits and clothes. This was going to be a huge opening in Australia, the start of a country-wide tour, and Dick decided to look really smart for it.

'So before we left for Australia, Dick said to me: "I think I'll have a special dinner suit made up. Will you get Giuseppe to bring some material round." The tailor went round to Dick's dressing room at the BBC and Dick picked out what he wanted. He never had a fitting, as Giuseppe had made so many suits up over the years that no one thought twice about it.

'So now we were in Australia, backstage at the Sydney Opera House in Dick's dressing room, with twenty minutes to go before the curtain goes up. Dick got dressed and asked me: "How do I look?"

'"Wonderful," I told him. "But what about the trousers?"

'"Why?" he said, startled. "What's the matter with them?"

'"They're too short." And they were – at least four inches too short.

'"Jesus Christ!' Dick was aghast. "What am I going to do? Giuseppe's in London, we're in Australia and there's no time for a refit."

'"Actually, I think it's very funny," I said, and meant it. "I thought you'd done it deliberately."

'"No, but the last trousers he made were for one of my characters, so he must have used those measurements. It's not his fault and I'll just have to improvise."

'So he pulled his trousers down two inches below his waist, and to get the hem even closer to his shoes he went out onstage bent at the knees like an old man.

'He went through the whole act like that, hobbling around, and he even took his bow the same way. He was a rip-roaring success, but next day on the radio we tuned in to hear their top disc jockey giving an account of his night at the show.

'"Well, folks," he said. "I was at the Opera House last night and Jesus Christ, that Dick Emery's a funny man. Only thing is, I didn't realize he was a cripple! He's got a humpy back and everything!" Australians tend to be pretty forthright, don't they?

'When Dick heard it, I thought he'd hit the roof. Instead he nearly hit the floor – laughing.'

Subsequently Dick recorded six *Dick Emery Shows* in Sydney, all specially written with a local flavour that went down a treat. A stand-up comic named Len Lowe became Dick's straight man, and the writers flown out to keep the scripts up to scratch were his trusted old mates John Warren and John Singer. 'They were the best of all the writers Dick ever had,' Peter confirmed.

In addition, all the Emery series had been sold by the BBC to a local network and were screened nationwide.

The 'Little Pommy Bastard,' as they affectionately called Dick, became a local hero with an enormous following.

Part of his success may have been due to his very unusual, if not unique, approach to his shows that went down particularly well with the informal, friendly people of Australia.

Normally live variety was made up of singers, dancers and 'spesh' (speciality) acts filling the first half of the bill, with the star taking over after the interval and making the second half all his own.

Not Dick. He would open the show himself, one man strolling alone onto the stage in front of the curtains, indulging in a spot of informal chat with the audience and actually going down into the auditorium to shake the outstretched hands. Then it was back onstage to introduce the first act, during which he hastened back to his dressing room to get into his first costume.

Lampwick would emerge from the wings to get them laughing, make his exit, and while the next act was doing its stuff Dick would be backstage again, frantically changing into Mandy or Hettie or Bovver Boy.

'The changes were almost as exhausting as being out front,' Dick once declared. 'With two shows a night, I was hopping around like a madman. Often I'd turn down the star dressing room three floors up and go for a "hole in the wall" right next to the stage. When you realize I'm talking tights, high-heeled boots, dress, wig, fresh make-up and false eyelashes, you'll get an idea of what was involved with each new change.

'Speed was essential; there was never any time to sit down and relax. All I asked for was a screen for privacy, a basin and a jug of water, a bucket, table and chair and a mirror. Quite often that's just what I got.'

It was worth it. Even in small towns in the middle of nowhere in the Australian outback, the theatres were packed to the rafters. In return,

Dick gave it all he'd got. He loved his Aussie audiences and they loved him.

Having 'conquered' Australia, Dick moved on to New Zealand, where he was equally popular and became a regular at the Ace of Clubs, a nightclub in Auckland. This was followed by extensive tours of the North and South Islands. Everywhere he went he was greeted like a long-lost friend – as his face was so familiar from the TV, people really thought they knew him and couldn't wait to shake his hand.

Sometimes things got trickier, as happened on one tour planned with stopovers in Hong Kong, Singapore and Jakarta. Dick's schedule was as frantic as ever, with everything timed to the last minute and no allowance for anything to go amiss.

This was a big mistake. At Singapore Airport, he came across one of those officials whose mission in life is to make everything difficult for everyone else. 'This functionary,' Dick reported, curling his tongue around the word in distaste, 'refused to let me on the plane. "Too many luggage!" he kept shouting.

'Well, admittedly I had ten cases. And he insisted on opening all of them. I had to explain the dresses and women's shoes and Mandy's wigs that were all spread out on the counter for his inspection! Of course, I missed the wretched plane.'

The most galling thing of that whole sorry episode was that Dick, the 'complete professional', had to phone the club in New Zealand where he was booked and tell them he was going to miss opening night – which was already sold out. When he did finally get there, at least they understood – and gave him a standing ovation.

Back in England Dick was again overtaken by bad health. This time his eyesight began to fail. 'I think I'm going blind in one eye,' he whispered to Margaret one day in the small office in Baker Street from where she still ran his life. 'What am I going to do?'

'You've got to see a specialist,' she told him, stepping into her mother hen role with which there was no argument. The surgeon at Moorfields Eye Hospital diagnosed a cataract. 'You've got to leave it to ripen until we can operate,' he said.

'How long?' Dick asked.

'Several weeks,' was the reply.

In the mid-70s the cataract operation was not as fast and fearless as it is today. For Dick the waiting was pure agony, as of course he insisted on continuing to work. As his vision blurred and grew more faint, he felt he was squinting into the camera. Peter Elliott did his best to reassure him by making him laugh.

'Don't worry,' he said. 'If you go blind, you can still work onstage using a guide dog in a sequined jacket!'

'Thanks a lot, friend,' said Dick sarcastically.

The operation was successful. However, when the bandages were removed Dick found he had no focus, so for the rest of his life he had to wear contact lenses.

'Sometimes it could be a nightmare with the make-up, the heat of the lights and smoke-filled rooms. But eventually I got used to it, because I had to.' One year later the other eye became blurred and he had to go through the whole operation again.

Far more serious even than the fear of going blind was that once again his 'perfect' marriage was showing signs of wear. Too many separations, lonely nights, temptations, too many miles apart, too much hard work. Who knows? Dick's fifth marriage started to falter. This time he felt that he really had tried. In the beginning, Josephine had accompanied him on many of his tours and theatre dates but later they settled into a routine where Dick dashed here and there, while Josephine looked after their home and waited for him to come back. This he did less and less frequently, using his 'work' as an excuse. Josephine felt abandoned, and Dick resented being the one who kept everything going, but never had time to enjoy the benefits.

Dick felt terrible about the worsening situation, and once again he unburdened his heart on paper. His own words:

It is not depression, it is sadness that has totally enveloped me. Sad, because having reached this part of my life, with all the experiences I have had, there is no joy. No buoyancy, no lift to life any more. In defence I bury myself in work because it's the only thing that gives me any lift.

But Dick's spirits were given a tremendous lift in 1976 when, out of the blue, he was reunited with his long-lost first-born son, Gilbert. Dick's eyes filled with tears of delight every time he remembered.

'After we lost contact, I had no idea where he or his mother were. All Gilbert knew was that I was an entertainer, but he didn't know my name, where I was or what I was doing. He did, however, know that the GI his mother married was not his real father.

'From time to time, Gilbert made efforts to trace his origins. Eventually a letter found its way to me, and he identified himself with enough clues and facts to make me certain it really was him and not some crackpot joker.

'I telephoned him immediately – and that was it. We met in Blackpool when I was doing my show on the pier and he walked into my dressing room, grinned and said: "Hi, Dad!" After that we kept in touch all the time, and in 1977 he brought his wife Kathleen over from the States so they could both join me on a tour of Ireland.

'As a surprise for me, and as a very good publicity stunt, TV host Gay Byrne introduced Gilbert from the audience of an Irish TV chat show. For the watching viewers it was the son they never knew I had.' For Dick it was a heart-stopping, magical moment. And for Gilbert, by then an insurance official back home in the States, it was the end of a lifetime's search.

The papers called it 'the best-kept secret in show business'.

'I had no idea we were "going public," said Dick. 'But I was delighted to show my boy to the world, even if it was thirty years late! I mean, you only had to look at him to see he was my son by his eyes and grin and the fact that he laughed at my jokes. What more could a father want?'

Even Gilbert couldn't distract Dick from his work for long. The format for *The Dick Emery Show* was changing. The Interviewer was replaced by a series of sketches, each telling its own little story. The idea of one storyline incorporating several sketches, which is what Dick wanted, was still not acceptable to the BBC top brass.

The Bovver Boy, dressed in denim and boots, was always one of Dick's favourites. He allowed Dick to return to adolescence and be really naughty! With his con man father (played by Roy Kinnear) he was always up to mischief and endeared himself to countless fans with his catchphrase: 'Dad, I've got it wrong again.' A short sketch that appealed to Dick in the days when the Interviewer was still going strong, went as follows:

INTERVIEWER: May I ask how you earn your living, sir?

BOVVER BOY: Yer. I'm self-employed, ain't I?

INTERVIEWER: Oh really? And what exactly do you do?

BOVVER BOY: I'm in the 'uverwizell' business.

INTERVIEWER: The 'uverwizell' business? Could you perhaps explain that?

BOVVER BOY: Certainly. I go to a shopkeeper and he gives me five quid a week – 'uverwizell' kick his windows in!

Roy Kinnear remembered his screen 'son': 'There was no way either of us could take each other seriously. We each knew the tenuous hold we both had on the lines and we were both hoping fervently not to be the first to break up. The trouble was that the slightest twinkle in Dick's eye when I was having trouble with my lines meant I was on a hiding to nothing.'

Harold Snoad, who produced and directed Dick for eight years, had to hold everything together. No easy task when his actors were likely to dissolve into hysterical laughter at any moment, as when they were filming in 'Sherwood Forest'. Harold takes up the story:

'Actually it was a wood near Shepperton Studios,' he recalled. 'The sequence involved a period version of Bovver Boy and his dad, in which Dad was selling an elixir to protect customers from mortal injury.

'During the sketch we saw Dad prove to a potential customer how well it worked by apparently stabbing himself with a dagger without causing injury. The effect was very simply achieved by having a dagger with a blade that shot up into the handle when pressure was applied to the tip.

'We saw Dad explaining the scam to Bovver Boy and how the thing worked, then leaving him to demonstrate to the customers. Along comes a potential client and Bovver Boy goes into his sales patter. But when he used it on his own arm, the whole thing sprang apart with the various parts scattering in all directions and the spring actually hitting him on the nose!'

A perfect cue for 'Dad, I've got it wrong again,' as everyone burst out laughing. Except this time the mistake was a real mistake, and inspired Harold to save all the funny 'unscheduled' moments, which he called *The Comedy of Errors*. This was shown to the studio audience on recording days, and they loved it. Even Dick, who generally hated watching himself perform, loved *The Comedy of Errors* when he could watch and chuckle at the marvellous moments when it all went hilariously wrong.

'I loved that show,' he chortled. 'I mean, if you can't laugh at yourself – who can you laugh at?'

Once again, Dick was off to the seaside for his summer show. Bert Weedon, 'that maestro of guitar-playing genius' as Dick introduced him onstage, was on the bill with him. They were old and good friends and Bert remembers their time together: 'We spent a lot a time in each other's dressing rooms, chatting, reminiscing and laughing about life in general. Dick used to entertain me with endless anecdotes, all told with the right accents and impressions.

'He would break off and suggest: "Play me something on your guitar, Bert." I would pick up the guitar and play him a few tunes, while he sat back in the corner listening and relaxing.

'At one point, when we were facing up to a long seaside summer together, working twice nightly for months, he asked me to help him choose a guitar. "Pick me out a good 'un, Bert. I want to learn to play the guitar if you'll teach me".

'I helped him choose a guitar, but I felt I should mention that the guitar is an instrument that demands diligent study and practice. His reply was straight to the point. "If you'll show me what to do and how to do it, I promise that I'll practise." "Actually, it's more of a lifetime study," I warned him. "In that case, the sooner we start the sooner I'll catch you up," he said with a chuckle. But I had a feeling that he meant it.

'Throughout that run I went into his dressing room every night and we'd both get our guitars out and strum together. I showed him a few moves and he watched me like a hawk – and sure enough, the next night he would have mastered completely what I'd shown him the evening before. Truly amazing!

'He would have every finger movement and note off to perfection.

Then he'd look up at me with that big grin and say: "What about that, then, mate?" That was Dick!'

Dick admitted that he preferred summer shows but felt pantomime was an essential part of his public image. In 1977, he performed in panto for the last time. It was *Cinderella* in Leeds. Now that he was in demand overseas, the thought of the sun in the southern hemisphere compared to the bleak British winter was too tempting to ignore. It also gave him an excuse to run away from marriage number five, which was fading fast. No matter how hard he tried he couldn't rekindle the delight he had felt for his beautiful wife and luxurious home. Again he committed his feelings to paper:

I have trod those well-worn paths of anguish, felt bleeding from the sharp stones of conscience. Pricked by doubts and fears of unknown enemies of happiness. They say to love is for fools. But is it foolish to have known love? Is it foolish to shed the salty tears of a child when love is denied by death or departure? No, my friends, for love transcends all other earthly things. For to have loved is to have known.

Restored by the sheer hard work of the shows and non-stop social life in Australia, Dick soon recovered his equilibrium and fell in love once more. He was so infatuated with his latest conquest that he even considered emigrating to Australia and setting up home with her there for good. 'This lasted for almost a year,' he told me later. 'Until I came home unexpectedly one day and found her in bed with someone else. The other person wasn't a man but another woman. I didn't know whether to laugh or cry.

'So I just kept on working and as usual managed to forget everything else. And then out of the blue I was asked to write a cookery book, *Dick Emery's Cookbook* – but of course they didn't really want Dick Emery, they wanted recipes from their favourite characters.'

So Lampwick obliged with 'Shell Shock Stew', 'Dumplin Reinforcements', 'Luvly Leg o' Pork' and 'Bread Puddin', while Ton-Up Boy rode in with 'Tater Straws', 'Pumpkin Scones' and 'Fish 'n' Chips' ('ideal food for bikers cause they also keeps you warm when stuffed up yer jacket!').

Clarence ('I've had some lovely tarts in my time') greeted his Honky

Tonk diners with such delicacies as 'Honey Fruit Pie', 'Sultana Lemon Delicious' and (naturally) his own special 'Spotted Dick'.

The Vicar produced soul food like: 'Heavenly Raspberry Soufflé' and 'Coffee Cake Offering', while Mandy chose 'Some of the recipes that were favourites with my seven husbands'. They included: 'Raspberry Fool' ('there's no fool like a Raspberry Fool, is there?'), 'Poached Polka Dots' and 'Lobster Paella a là Michael' ('I wonder who Michael is? I bet he's awful. But I know I'd like him!').

The cookbook became a great favourite all over Australia. But now Dick had nothing to keep him from returning to England, where he redoubled his efforts to win back Josephine.

He sent her flowers every week and called her every day, and even took her on a romantic holiday for two to Paris, where he did everything he could to recapture the old magic. For a little while he thought all would be well, but once he was off on tour again, the rows and resentment returned. Absence was not making the heart grow fonder, and although he couldn't bring himself to confront the problem, he knew their relationship was deteriorating and that he was living a lie.

22. And Then There Was Me

'A sister for Mandy?'

FAY

And that's how I found him in January 1979 at Ealing Film Studios. Lonely, sad and disillusioned. He put on such a brave face in public that only his very closest friends knew how his heart was breaking. Dick's life once again centred on his work and he drove himself harder and faster than ever. This was taking its toll on his health and right from the start I realized he was pushing himself too hard. Shortness of breath, a sudden stabbing pain and a general restlessness were the giveaway signs. But he wouldn't talk about it.

Our endless cups of coffee and chats had gone on for several weeks when, out of the blue, Dick declared: 'I'm going to America for a month; they might be interested in *The Dick Emery Show* over there.' He sounded really excited and I knew he was keen to follow the success that Benny Hill had achieved in America. 'Josephine wants to come with me, so I'm taking her,' he added abruptly.

'Fine,' I answered with an unexpected stab of heartache. It took me by surprise as Dick and I had never done more than talk, and although we both felt real affection for each other we had exchanged no more than a kiss on the cheek in greeting. I think we were both fooling ourselves that we could save our marriages as long as we had each other for support.

So, off Dick went, and although I missed him I got on with my life as usual. Within twenty-four hours I received the first of his phone calls, which continued from everywhere he stopped right across America. He must have missed me too!

Between small parts in TV shows and occasional theatre dates I used to work as a model, and there was always plenty of modelling work in

April during London Fashion Week. I was on the catwalk, showing a collection for a German designer at the Inn on the Park in Central London when, to my astonishment, I saw Dick's head pop out from behind a pillar. How I managed to keep walking without falling off I can't imagine. Back in the dressing room I thought I must have imagined him, but as I stepped out in the next garment, there he was again, beaming at me and making frantic hand signals, which I took to mean he would be waiting in the bar. I gave him an imperceptible nod and got through the rest of the show with great difficulty.

At last, the final outfit shown, I was free to go and see him. I hadn't realized how much I'd missed him and he seemed to feel the same way. It was difficult not to run into each other's arms, but we were in public and everyone knew who he was. We sat on our bar stools and ordered a drink. After one sip he said: 'Let's go for a drive and a chat. I'll die unless I can touch you.' There wasn't much point in pretending any more; his heart beat as loudly as mine and our kisses were so sweet, they obliterated rational thought.

Having an affair with a public figure is not at all easy. If one tries to have a private tryst in an out-of-the-way hotel, it's fairly disconcerting if one's lover, heavily disguised in dark glasses, cap and turned-up collar, is asked for his autograph while signing the register as Mr & Mrs Smith! A sense of humour is vital to avoid turning romantic meetings into sordid scrambles. But we managed. I couldn't possibly deny the sexual attraction but that was only part of what pulled us together. As our relationship grew we understood each other completely. There was no need for words and when we did speak we said the same thing at exactly the same time!

So many people all round the world found Dick fascinating, it's hardly surprising that I did too. What did surprise me was that the feeling was mutual. Why he chose me has always puzzled me. In hindsight I think he may have been attracted to my maternal instinct. I seem to collect wounded animals and lonely people, and he was certainly wounded and lonely, and although we shared lots of fun, laughter and excitement, my role with him was really as carer and comforter. But that wasn't so obvious at the beginning of our relationship.

I had acted in several episodes of Bernie Winter's TV series, when

Bernie asked me if I would like a part in his 1979 summer show in Great Yarmouth.

Before committing myself to this, I mentioned it to Dick who thought it was a super idea, as by pure chance he was also playing Great Yarmouth that year. So fate seemed to be keeping us together, and our feelings grew stronger all the time.

By Christmas we knew we had to do something about it. We had spent so much time together and were both so miserable when apart, but neither of us wanted to hurt our partners and the thought of uprooting family and facing the Press made us postpone the inevitable. Instead, we 'escaped' to the southern hemisphere.

Because my husband and I were often working away from home, the top floor of our house had been converted into a self-contained flat for a housekeeper who ran everything very efficiently and took over the cooking in my absence.

My mother lived with us for most of the year and stepped into my shoes when I was away filming or doing a show, usually only for one or two nights at a time. But in the summer the shows would last several months. The boys loved to join me for their holidays in whichever seaside resort I was playing. So no one was surprised when I said I had a tour of New Zealand and Australia over Christmas.

To say I had a guilty conscience would be putting it mildly. I was wracked with guilt but I really believed I couldn't live without Dick and he had told me that he couldn't live without me. So I allowed myself to be swept along like a piece of straw in a torrent of rain. That's exactly what it felt like.

After a twenty-four hour flight, during which I sat next to a woman who was so scared she insisted on holding my hand all the way, I arrived in Auckland, where Dick met me at the airport. As usual we had flown at separate times to avoid press interest.

And so I became part of the Dick Emery team. With no other commitments or family pressures we could concentrate on each other and it was fantastic, though very hard work. Although we were wonderfully looked after and organized by Tony Goodliffe, Phill Warren and our road manager, whom we called Billy the Roady, Dick's schedule was exhausting, even without carrying the burden of responsibility for the show. We travelled all day and worked all night, with time in between to pack, unpack and maintain costumes, wigs and props. If we were lucky, we would find somewhere still open after the show for a meal, and if we were very lucky our hotel would be quiet enough in the morning for a few more hours' precious sleep.

When I first started to tour with Dick, all I did was sit in his dressing room and watch as he laid out his make-up, set up his wigs and put costumes and shoes in the right order for his quick changes. But as time progressed, he trusted me to help him and before long I was allowed to do it on my own. This was excellent as it meant he could have an extra half hour with his feet up before the show. Peter Elliott generally came out for the start of a tour to make sure everything was OK, but once he left we could run into all sorts of trouble. For instance, there might be no steps from the stage to the auditorium, so Dick couldn't go and shake hands for his opening, or no water, light, chairs, etc. in the dressing rooms. Sometimes, there were greater problems, like no musicians or no stage lighting. Almost anything could and did happen, but by showtime everything had to be running without a hitch. And it always was.

In New Zealand, Dick had a wonderful group of acts and musicians around him who very soon became good friends and touring together was great fun. After a few weeks we had worked our way down to Invercargill, the most southerly town on the South Island. We were working in a club that had no dressing rooms at all, so the manager had donated his office for the evening. I had just finished packing Mandy's glittery frock into the skip and, looking round to see what else was ready to go, I found Dick kneeling on the carpet staring up at me with an expression in those intense hazel eyes that froze me to the spot.

'Will you marry me?' he asked, reaching out for my hand. The joy I felt at that moment made me forget every sorrow I had ever known or fear of what might lie ahead. Without stopping to think, I whispered: 'Yes, I will, I'd love to.'

Dick invited everyone in the show out for a meal and told them our news. The congratulations and euphoria of that magical evening almost made us forget one thing. We were both still married to other people and until the situation was resolved, we knew we would be instant fodder for the tabloids, which was something neither of us could bear to think about.

How could we have guessed that ultimately a more terrible and final tragedy than having our love sullied and sensationalized, and our lives held up for public scrutiny, would one day separate him from me for ever?

I said 'yes' that evening and I meant it. But I never did marry Dick.

This was the first of three tours we did together in New Zealand. We played every town big enough to have a theatre or club and enjoyed every moment of it. Well, nearly every moment. There were one or two episodes that took a bit of manoeuvring. There was a car company which was very keen for Dick to use one of their cars for his tour. Excellent publicity for them and a free car for Dick. No problem. But I shared the driving with Dick and on one of my 'turns', a door fell off a lorry in front of us and smashed the bonnet of our car. Dick couldn't make up his mind which was worse, to admit he had let someone else drive the car or to say he was driving but couldn't avoid the smash. His manly pride won the day and he admitted that I was driving. No one seemed too concerned.

When we arrived at Rotarua, the sulphur in the air from the local boiling mud pools, which smells exactly like bad eggs, was so strong that every time Dick took a breath to sing he choked and tears poured down his face. A local tried to comfort him: 'Don't worry, in a week you won't even notice it.' We were only there for two nights and Dick had to 'speak' his songs.

In Wellington, the crisis was more serious. We had flown in, but the skip containing all the costumes had not flown in with us. After several frantic phone calls we located the skip over a hundred miles away, sitting on the edge of an airfield. With two hours before curtain up, things didn't look good but after a few more calls, and with the assistance of a helicopter and two taxis, we retrieved the skip and Dick took the stage on time.

The people of New Zealand were very friendly. They loved Dick from his TV shows but even more in the theatre. There weren't many live performances on offer and they really appreciated Dick. And he loved them in return.

Once the tour was running smoothly, Dick suggested that I should join him onstage in a couple of sketches. I was never bored by being in the dressing room or in my supporting role, but to be able to work with

Dick was very exciting. We wrote and rehearsed a little sketch that started with Dick onstage as himself. I came on as Mademoiselle Fifi, a French friend of his from Paris, we did a few gags and then he remembered something he had to go and do. He asked the band, who were usually on the stage with us, if they would play some music for me until he came back. They started with 'Under the Bridges of Paris' but soon broke into 'The Stripper'. On hearing the music I began to dance and slowly peeled off one glove and then another . . . Dick had had a beautiful black dress made for me with diamanté all over it. Underneath I wore a corset and black stockings. Very high heels, long gloves and a feather boa completed the outfit. By the time I got as far as undoing the dress (which was done up with Velcro) Mandy came onstage and tried to join in but when I opened my dress with a great flourish, she couldn't open hers so she got very annoyed and chased me off the stage, at the last moment lifting her dress at the back to reveal Union Jack knickers! It was really very simple, but the audience loved it. Word went around that there were two strippers in the show and soon the already full houses became packed even tighter. The other sketch was with the Vicar and an organist. I'll leave the rest to your imagination!

Life was even more hectic when I was performing as well as helping backstage. Dick and I shared a dressing room and I soon learnt when to encourage, when to shut up, when to help and always to laugh. By the time our tour ended in New Zealand we had become the perfect team, looking forward to opening in Australia. First stop Sydney.

Before we left the beautiful islands of New Zealand, Dick was given a Maori gala dinner. When we arrived at the beach, we were greeted with a Haka (the Maori war dance that they do here before Rugby matches). In New Zealand it is saved for very special occasions and Dick was honoured. Dancing in traditional costume, the Maoris were awe-inspiring. The meal was called a Hungi, which is a kind of barbecue. A huge bonfire was lit on the beach with several round stones thrown into it to get hot. Meanwhile a large pit was dug by the fire. Then the hot stones were placed in the bottom of the pit, the food wrapped in palm leaves and placed on the hot stones and the pit was then filled in again with sand. Hours later it was dug up and the food was as tender and sweet as anything we had ever tasted.

We spent a wonderful evening watching them dance and joining in with their melodious singing. A perfect way to say goodbye to the Land of the Long White Cloud.

Australia was a whole new ball game with a faster way of life, especially in Sydney and the other big cities. But in the bush it was like stepping back in time with wooden theatres that had terrific character, but not much in the way of comfort. The welcome was always wonderful. Dick was mobbed by adoring fans wherever he went and I felt it was a privilege to watch and be part of it all! Again the organization was superb thanks to Dennis Smith. Robert Finikiotis looked after Dick's financial affairs and he and his wife Jenny became our good friends. Our road manager was again called Billy and looked after us like a mother hen.

After a few weeks in Sydney, we started a tour that would take us from coast to coast of Australia and to Tasmania. Up at the Gold Coast in the north-east the temperature was often 120 degrees. With no air conditioning backstage, keeping the make-up on was a problem, and with Dick's fast changes it was a nightmare. If we opened a window insects came in in swarms. If we shut the window, Mandy's eyelashes floated down her cheeks and we had to wring her wig out like a sponge. Lampwick couldn't get his moustache to stick and the Vicar nearly fainted inside his dog collar! Then there were the snakes and spiders. There was always a chance of finding a Redback (a deadly poisonous spider) in your costume or of being temporarily blinded by a frog that spat venom at you and seemed particularly fond of lurking near the Stage Door.

The one thing which marred Dick's pleasure was that since his heart attack he was not allowed to fly, unless accompanied by a qualified pilot. So he planned to get me to pass my flying test so we could go up together in a Tiger Moth (which is only a two-seater). In New Zealand and Australia people in rural areas use planes as we use cars. There are such huge distances to cover and the weather is so good, it's the obvious choice. It was not at all unusual to own a two- or four-seater plane with a little grass runway, or 'strip', as they called it. Even the smaller towns had a flying club with plenty of planes and instructors for hire. So Dick's plan for my instruction was started in New Zealand and continued all over Australia. I was willing but not quick to learn. Terror frequently overcame me and when I'm scared I go deaf so I couldn't understand the instructor! However, we persevered and gradually I improved. I'm not naturally fond of machines – I had to take my driving test three times – but Dick was optimistic.

On one occasion I was told to practise stalling – and getting out of it. The idea is that you go up to three thousand feet, stall your engine, then get the nose down so you build up speed and hope to God the engine will start again. You have to remember so much at the same time as you're doing this tricky exercise – not to slip to the side, noting your 'carb heat' (carburettor temperature), a whole manual . . .

For some reason, on this day, something didn't work. Inside the cabin we steamed up with condensation and water was dripping everywhere.

As well as being optimistic, Dick was brave, and generally sat in the back of the four-seater Piper Cherokee that was my usual plane. On this occasion the instructor and Dick were still smiling as I made a somewhat bumpy landing. But when we opened the doors to get out, we were surrounded by the Press and TV cameras. The media had been tipped off and were out in force. As we clambered out, someone laughed and pointed. It was then that I noticed the whole of the front of Dick's trousers were soaked. You can guess the rest. There was a shout: 'Gawd, look at that! She scared him so much he's wet himself!'

I tried to protest and explain about the condensation but no one was listening. The word went round; I never lived it down, nor did Dick! We continued to tour and I continued to learn and by the time we got to Perth on the West Coast, I had become a lot more confident and even started to enjoy it.

But when Dick and some new-found flying pals from Perth's flying club decided to liven up the place with a 'fly past', I decided discretion was definitely the better part of valour. So on a quiet Sunday morning, I watched Dick, kitted out in full flying gear, helmet and goggles, being offered a Tiger Moth with co-pilot for his pleasure. Someone else flew in a Chipmunk and other daredevils were in an assortment of vintage planes. Dick and Co buzzed the whole of Perth – at two hundred feet. 'Most of the population seem to take to their gardens for a family barbecue on Sundays and I could see their reaction,' Dick told me when he landed. 'They were furious! I could see them hopping up and down on their lawns, shaking their fists in the air.'

It was all in the papers next day. 'Dick Emery Buzzes Perth!' It was pure devilment, just for fun – they were all schoolboys at heart and it made a lovely memory for Dick.

One of my favourite memories was when we were in Ballarat, an old mining town. No more gold there today, but tourists are encouraged to take a sieve and 'pan' for gold in a stream. We all panned away un-successfully for a few minutes, getting very excited if we saw the tiniest fleck of glitter in the sandy water. Dick was a little distance upstream from me, and to this day I don't know how he did it, but suddenly I saw a big glint in my sieve and yelling with delight I pulled a gold chain from the murky depths. Of course I knew he must have arranged it. It was just the kind of sweet surprise that he loved to give.

As with all good things our wonderful tour came to an end and we had to return to England. The worst thought was knowing our time together would be limited and secret until we had worked out what to do.

I couldn't continue with the lie I was living and after agonizing for weeks, I decided to tell my husband that I wanted a separation. I intended to buy a small flat in London and wait until Dick had sorted himself out before thinking further. My husband was understandably furious and left England to pursue his career abroad. This left me to sell our house and make proper arrangements for my boys, mother and our numerous animals, including the boys' ponies. The housekeeper had to be found a new position and it was all very traumatic and difficult.

Dick told me he had broached the subject of divorce with Josephine and that was proving difficult too.

Meanwhile we continued to spend as much time as we could together, on the set when Dick was filming, and on tour around England and all over Ireland. Inevitably, the Press did find out and all hell broke loose. Every newspaper carried a story about how Dick had loved and left his women and lewd photos. Morecambe and Wise rushed about their TV studios sobbing noisily: 'Dick Emery's left me!' and we were held up for public scrutiny in a big way. Neither of us were proud of what we were doing – but we couldn't stop.

I was still living in the house in Farnham when there was a ring on the doorbell. There stood Dick, armed with only a suitcase and a forlorn expression.

'My wife's thrown me out,' he said without even a good-morning-how-are-you. 'Can I stay? I don't want the papers getting hold of it.' I still had my sons and mother living with me, although the housekeeper had gone by then. I couldn't possibly compromise my family by having Dick share my bedroom. There was only one solution. 'You can stay in the flat,' I said, 'but you must promise to behave. No creeping about in the night!' He agreed and was as good as his word, the perfect gentleman. Mother and the boys accepted him happily.

But after two weeks of seeing his sad face across the dining-room table at breakfast every morning – Dick could milk a scene for pathos like nobody else – I finally relented. That night I put on one of my French maid stage costumes, stacked a tray from the kitchen with a bottle of chilled champagne and two flute glasses, and tiptoed up the forbidden staircase to surprise him. It was really a joke to cheer him up but at that moment my mother's bedroom door opened and her enquiring face appeared.

'Fay! What *are* you doing?'

'Er—' thinking fast – 'just rehearsing for the *Benny Hill Show*, Mother.' I had actually worked with Benny and she had seen me playing the Merry Widow in one of his sketches.

'Well, don't stay up too late, dear,' she said, quietly closing the door.

To her great credit she never mentioned the incident again!

Dick lived with us for several months and when I told him of my plan to buy a flat, he wouldn't hear of it. After being together for so long why would I want to live alone? He just couldn't understand that I was trying not to push him. In the end I gave in and he bought the flat in St John's Wood. There was very little room for our 'things'. I put practically everything into storage and Dick brought just his clothes and a few bits to go on with. Moving from a nine-bedroom house, with plenty of room for everything, stables, swimming pool and housekeeper, into a tiny flat, living out of a suitcase while on tour, and trying not to neglect my family, would have been a nightmare if I hadn't been doing it with Dick. He was having his own problems trying to negotiate his divorce, leaving his dream house and all it meant to him and having to work all the time. Our favourite saying to each other in the worst moments was: 'I must be mad to love you this much!'

I was alone in the flat three weeks after we moved in, when the phone rang. It was Dick, sounding terrible. 'I'm going back to Josephine,' he said. I thought I'd misheard him.

'What did you say?'

'I can't do this, I'm going back to Jo.'

My heart stopped beating. 'Oh,' was all I could say and put the phone down. What had I done? Disrupted my poor family, gone through months of upheaval, given my heart trustingly to this man and now he had changed his mind! How could he?

I paced around the flat, but you couldn't take more than seven steps one way and nine the other. I had to get out. I walked all around Regent's Park without seeing anything. I bought a paper and sat on a bench to read it, not really knowing what I was doing. I didn't realize it was raining until the paper melted and fell in half. I went back to the flat, cold, wet and heartbroken. Margaret phoned and tried to comfort me and talk some sense into me. It didn't work. I lay all night on 'our' bed, looking at the ceiling and wondering how to draw the next breath. I didn't know this was Dick's usual behaviour. I'd never met anyone who could change their mind so completely.

I had been very sad when I split up with my husband, sad to hurt him, sad for the children, sad for the dream that hadn't worked. But I had known it wasn't working long before I met Dick, and even though he probably goaded me into action sooner than I had intended, I'm afraid my marriage wouldn't have survived anyway. Dick had told me many times that it was exactly the same for him. Knowing that he had lived with another woman for a year in Australia, I saw no reason to doubt him. And now this.

I went to stay with a friend for a few days and cried non-stop. Everyone was very kind and supportive but didn't seem nearly as surprised as I was. I was devastated and couldn't see how I was going to start again, without Dick. Luckily both my boys were on holiday with their father so they didn't have to live through it – they had grown to love Dick and would miss him. My mother had retired to her cottage in

Cornwall. Although she was always loving and tolerant with me, she didn't approve of 'living in sin' and I know she suffered too. I had understood from Dick that Josephine didn't care for him at all any more, but I think he was wrong, she too was hurt. We had done so much damage and all for nothing.

Six days later the phone rang at four o'clock in the morning. 'It's me,' whispered Dick. 'I must see you, can I come round?'

My heart started beating again. 'Of course,' I said. 'It's your flat.' I was trying to be angry with him but when I saw him, he looked so terrible all I could do was hug him and love him just as much as before. He wanted to come back 'for ever'.

We rebuilt our lives, made new promises, new plans and continued to work, work, work. The BBC had at last agreed to launch a new series for Dick called *Legacy of Murder*. For years he had dreamed of making a comedy thriller with a cliff-hanger each week to keep the public in suspense until the next episode. The theme was a complete departure from Dick's public persona, with his new main character being Bernie Weinstock, a seedy Jewish detective. Dick spent months practising the accent and mannerisms, listening to tapes and talking to anyone who might be useful. There were plenty of opportunities for the old favourite characters, who popped up all the time. Filming took the unit to Paris, Tunis and across England for atmospheric locations.

We had such fun in between the gruelling work schedule, shared so many laughs and overcame numerous near disasters – including rescuing me from a runaway camel in Tunisia – that I was quite unprepared for the next time Dick 'went back to Josephine'. He just couldn't cope with the number of times he had married and broken up. This time at least I had a little hope that he would come back. And only twenty-four hours later he was on the phone again. On the last occasion we parted, I actually sent him away, unable to bear to watch him tearing himself apart. I was determined to be strong-minded and rented a flat for myself – but on the evening I moved in, he moved in with me.

After years of friendship with Peter Elliott as his manager, Dick decided it was time for a change. Another old friend, Tony Lewis, was delighted to take him on, but sadly they had only two years together. Tony remembers: 'Dick was one of the most loved and respected artists of his era, not only by his public, but also by many people in the same profession all over the world. He could make me laugh just by telling me the time!'

Over the next two years we travelled thousands of miles all around the world. To America to see Gilbert, to Majorca for a holiday, all over Europe filming for the BBC and back to New Zealand and Australia twice. From top to toe of Britain and Ireland, to Fiji, Borneo and Dubai. We were together twenty-four hours a day, living the lives of nomads, and we laughed our way through every crisis. It didn't matter to us that Dick was considerably older than me – or that I was considerably taller than him. All that mattered was that we loved each other and were together.

But all the love in the world couldn't help Dick early in 1982 when we were again in Perth, Western Australia. Dick's health was clearly deteriorating, and I was getting more concerned week by week as I watched him battle with his body. He actually took his weights on tour and worked out every day – the porters could have been straight out of one of his sketches as they tried to hump that particular bag. 'Wait for it!' Dick would whisper to me. 'He's almost there. *Now!*' And he'd give vent to a wheezy chuckle. Dick himself turned purple with his own efforts, but he wouldn't stop. Pure determination kept him going at a breakneck pace.

On the day that was to prove so fateful we had attended a Variety Club lunch, then Dick had spent the afternoon handing out meals on wheels. The elderly were ecstatic to meet him and it all took longer than planned. We only had time to rush back to our hotel for a quick shower before setting off for the club where Dick was appearing that night.

I listened to Dick singing in the shower but his voice didn't sound normal, so I rushed in to investigate. He was very ill. His lungs were full of fluid because of his heart condition. He found he could breathe better in the steam and was determined to be well enough to do the show. So he was trying to rehearse his songs!

I called the hotel doctor, who said Dick must stay in bed. But I had to lock him in while I went to see about cancelling the show. The next day we found a specialist, who told me to get him home to England and to his own doctors at once. Definitely no more work. Having to cancel the show, and the end of the tour, was Dick's worst nightmare. He thought he was letting down not only the public but also his fellow actors. I assured him that everyone understood and wished him a speedy recovery, but he was hardly comforted.

My nightmare was getting him home safely. It was such a long flight and we weren't sure how the pressure would affect him. But we made it.

Back in England he improved. But the fumes in London were not helping him. One weekend we hired a boat and with his son Michael and my son Nick we went for a cruise down the Thames. We had just gone through Shepperton Lock when we saw a charming riverside bungalow in a huge garden full of trees. There was a FOR SALE board up. 'Wouldn't it be lovely to live by the river,' sighed Dick. I wrote down the number on the board and a couple of months later we bought it and moved in.

Dick was in his element, he loved pottering about 'fixing' things and planning our new décor. But best of all for him was strolling by the river, it was so peaceful and a very good place to relax away from the hustle and bustle of the world.

The BBC was so pleased by the success of the first comedy thriller series, that they commissioned another for 1982. This time it was called *Jack of Diamonds*, with actor Tony Selby brought in as Bernie Weinstock's assistant. 'There was a marvellous atmosphere among the cast and crew,' Tony recalled. 'I was always a fan, but I found out from working with Dick that he was a brilliant actor; his characterization was superb, he actually became the Vicar or Lampwick, etc . . . from the very centre of his being.'

Filming took us to Amsterdam on location and up and down the country once more. Dick was on medication to help his heart and I watched him like a hawk. Sometimes I would see him pale under his make-up so I popped a pill into my mouth, then rushed up to give him a kiss so transferring the pill into his mouth without anyone knowing what was going on. They just thought I was besotted with him, which was true. No one knew how he groaned in pain in his dressing room, how increasingly difficult it was for him to remember his lines. How tired he was or how hard he fought to carry onto the end of his series. With the last footage safely in the can, we retired to Shepperton to recuperate. But not for long. He had theatre dates and insisted on fulfilling them.

Sometimes he was so ill that I had to drive him to the venue, do his make-up, dress him and literally push him onto the stage, whispering his opening line to him as he went. 'Are you sure you want to do this?' I frequently asked him. 'Bills to pay,' he would wheeze back. 'To hell with the bills, what about you, us?' 'I'll manage, if I can just get this show over, then I'll rest.' But there was always another show. In between, when he felt better for a few days, we made the most of our 'love nest', as the papers referred to it later. Dick was really happy in our bungalow. We made friends with our next-door neighbours and in the village of Shepperton, where Dick turned a trip to the supermarket into a riot. We saw more of Dick's children, whom he loved and missed very much. We now had room to invite them over for meals, which made him very happy. His and my children got on extremely well.

Dick particularly enjoyed entertaining the dustbin men. I would find them all sitting in the kitchen. He would tell them stories, keeping them in stitches while he made them tea and conned them into eating the jam tarts he made by the dozen whenever he needed a little occupational therapy! They looked good but were often so hard you could easily break a tooth on them, though no one minded. In November we had a bonfire party in our garden for family and neighbours. Dick seemed fairly well and ran about with sparklers like a boy.

He knew how much I loved cats and made secret phone calls until he located a black Burmese kitten. He insisted that I drive him (by now he couldn't drive himself because the effort made him short of breath) to an unknown location where I was presented with not only the adorable kitten, but food, litter, bed and everything I could possibly need. That was so typically Dick, even when he was so very ill he never did things by halves.

23. The Final Hours

'We can't have that!'

DIANA DORS

Like so many things in life it all happened very dramatically. One moment we were together at our riverside home, planning the Christmas festivities. The next he was in hospital, never to come out. It would be the worst Christmas I could ever know.

A few days before Christmas, Dick began shouting in pain, crying out loud because it was too much to bear. Yet he still refused to let me call a doctor.

'I'll be all right,' he gasped, rocking in pain. Later we found out that his liver had swollen to five times as large as it should have been – even now I can't begin to imagine the agony he must have been enduring.

Normal life became impossible. He begged me: 'Don't go to sleep, Fay! Don't leave me. If you sleep you're leaving me, and I need you.' So I stayed awake as long as he did.

I had to be there to hold him, kiss him, do anything to let him know he had my strength and my life force to call on. Then he could sleep – but only for a few minutes at a time before the pain woke him again.

Eventually I managed to call Margaret Thomas. Dick had drifted into an uneasy sleep. I slipped out of the bedroom, and phoned her from the living room.

'Margaret, we've got to do something—'

'Leave it to me.' She understood immediately, and made an emergency call.

The doctor was adamant. 'Bring him to the Cromwell Hospital right away. I will be ready there to receive him.'

For once, Dick went meekly along with it.

239

I got him into his clothes, because he couldn't dress himself. I drove like a demon, because I knew the quicker I could get him there, the quicker they could give him something to ease his pain. The journey took forty-five minutes and throughout that nightmare drive Dick gripped the dashboard until his knuckles turned white, uttering soft moans at every bump in the road.

They gave him a private room and that night I slept in a chair next to his bed. The next night was Christmas Eve and I drove back home to pack a few things for him, plus a small case for myself.

They were playing carols on the car radio and I imagined families all across the land who would soon be opening presents around the Christmas tree, preparing the turkey, greeting relatives and friends. The Queen would give her traditional Christmas message on TV at 3.00 p.m. as usual. How could everything be so normal?

I had stacked all our own presents under the tree in the living room and when I got home I packed them carefully into a black bin liner to take back to the hospital next day. We would open them together.

I dropped into bed, exhausted, with the curious emptiness of knowing it was the first time I had slept without Dick in that house. The phone rang at 6.00 a.m. on Christmas morning.

A woman's voice said: 'Mr Emery has been moved into Intensive Care. Can you please get here at once?'

I threw our cases and presents into the car and woke my neighbours asking them to look after my kitten, then broke more rules of the Highway Code that frosty morning to get to him. In an Intensive Care room, Dick was half sitting, half lying in bed, taking oxygen from two small plastic tubes up either nostril. His bare arms had more tubes in the veins, but at least he could move them.

The day started to take on a crazy note when the nurse, in all innocence, announced my arrival: 'Mr Emery, your daughter's come to see you!'

My first thought was: 'Oh God, that's the last thing we need! I don't want Dick to be upset or insulted.'

I needn't have worried. Dick merely turned his head to her with a big smile, and said: 'Actually, she's my granddaughter!' That was good. At least he could still laugh.

I leant over the bed, and said gently: 'Darling, is there anything you want? What can I do to help you?'

He struggled to speak. Then sharply: 'For a start, you can catch those seagulls!' I really didn't know if he was trying to be funny. There wasn't a gull in sight, of course.

But he persisted: 'They're coming to get me! I can't stand it.'

I looked at the nurse, and she gave me a little nod, the kind that meant: *Humour him.* He was short of oxygen and hallucinating. And I realized in that moment that Dick was genuinely terrified and thought the seagulls he could see were flying towards him intent on pecking his eyes out!

So I jumped around the room flapping at non-existent seagulls, catching them, and cramming them into a plastic bag.

'There, they've gone now. They won't be back,' I assured him.

'Promise?' A weak voice from the pillow.

'Promise!'

Dick watched my every move and as long as I kept doing it he was perfectly happy. Occasionally I 'missed one', and he'd duck his head and shout hoarsely: 'You missed it! Get it, quick!'

Dashing around the room, trying to avoid tripping over the chairs and wires and the medical equipment to grab the invisible seagulls, I found myself laughing and crying at the same time at the sheer stupidity of it.

If it were written into one of Dick's farces, no one would have believed it.

Finally, after an hour, Dick was exhausted and fell asleep. Now quiet, he gathered his strength and reserved his oxygen – so that the next time he came to the surface his brain was clear – and he was sensible again.

In one of those sane moments he beckoned me over and took my hand. Looking up at me intently, he said: 'Fay, you know what I want most now – for both of us?'

'Tell me—'

'I want to take the worry out of your eyes. I can see the anxiety in them, and that makes me sad. Try not to worry. Please—'

I remembered later that he had written that line in a letter to me when he came back to me for the final time. *Take the worry out of your eyes . . .* I'm not that good an actress.

Later, on Christmas night, Dick finally fell into a drugged sleep. A nurse gently asked me to leave his bedside and offered me his private room on the floor above for the night. I was only too grateful to accept – until I saw the sack of presents which he hadn't opened and his clothes hanging in a cupboard. His favourite brown corduroy jacket was there, and I buried my face in it and cried silently for endless minutes before crawling onto his high hospital bed and trying to snatch some sleep.

Despite that dreadful time of waiting, hoping, and wondering, there were lighter moments when Dick rallied.

Incorrigible as ever, he could not ignore the plump arms of the nurses as they stretched across him to straighten his sheets – and could not refrain from kissing them either, to the accompaniment of scolding squeals and much laughter.

'*Please*, Mr Emery—'

I have no idea what the sound of uncontrollable hilarity from the Intensive Care unit did for anyone passing the door. But I like to think it worked wonders on the rest of the ward.

But then things took a turn for the worse. A very bad turn. Dick contracted a chest infection, and his heart was affected again. Three days after being admitted to the Cromwell Hospital, he was transferred to King's College. By now he was on a ventilator and had a drain in his chest, so moving him was very difficult.

In the ambulance they had to pump the air in by hand, squeezing a rubber bladder in and out like something out of a Victorian melodrama. Thank goodness he was unconscious and well out of it.

I tried to follow in my car – but found my way blocked by the hordes of Press who had been at the hospital ever since the news first broke. They were outside the main doors, watching the Accident & Emergency wing. And now, in the car park, they were swarming around my car like bees round a honeypot.

The melee became a scrum, with me in the middle.

Reporters and photographers jostled and elbowed each other to get at me, even sitting on the bonnet to stop me driving off as they shouted questions.

'How is he? What's his condition? Is he going to live?'

I screamed out: 'Get away from me! The man I love is in that ambulance and you're preventing me getting to him. He needs me!'

Finally I broke through, and chased after the ambulance. Somehow we got to the hospital at the same time. They whisked Dick onto a trolley, through the rubber doors of the Emergency entrance and into the lift.

He was taken straight to Intensive Care, several floors up, but the word was out. The Press were gathering and spent hours 'door-stepping', to use the Fleet Street term. I became a virtual prisoner up there on the sixth floor.

The uncertainty over Dick's health coupled with the tension and pressure of the media attention was turning me into a nervous wreck – and I couldn't leave Dick's side, because the Press tried all sorts of tricks to get a story. Two of them dressed up in white gowns and caps and wheeled a trolley with a third – the patient – fully dressed under a blanket. They got as far as Dick's room before they were challenged, by which time they'd had a peek through the little glass window to get their descriptive story for the next day's papers.

I suppose you have to admire their cheek – the whole country was waiting and wondering, with hourly bulletins on the radio as Dick's condition deteriorated. But at that moment it was the last thing I wanted – not just for myself, but for his children, Michael, Nick and Eliza, who found it an added burden to their distress when they came to visit their father.

The Intensive Care people were absolutely wonderful, both in the way they cared for Dick and in the concern they showed for his family, and me.

'Why don't you go home and get some rest?' the nurses said. 'I can't,' I responded. 'I need to be here, because I am willing him to get better. He is going to get better.' I made myself believe it, and they understood.

I'm afraid I don't like hospitals at the best of times. I hate the smell of disinfectant, let alone the sight of blood. The most terrifying thing is not knowing what's going on. Every time a buzzer went off or a light came on, I thought something had gone wrong and called a nurse over in a panic.

Those awful instruments reminded me of some kind of futuristic torture chamber from another planet, all chrome, steel and glass. Almost hidden away was one small plastic chair and I sat there holding his hand, hour after hour, day after day, until my head dropped onto the blanket beside him and I fell asleep from sheer exhaustion.

Since the first day in the Cromwell, one thing was certain: Dick didn't think he would die. And I was determined that he would live. So we never became too melodramatic over it. We talked about life, about loving one another, about his children and mine, and about our home and all we planned to do. In those endless hours in King's College I willed Dick as hard as I could to pull through, and time passed in a confused blur. He never fully regained consciousness. The seagulls were quiet. At least in his sedated slumber, Dick was at peace.

The truth is that if he had come round, he had so many tubes and pipes and holes in him, he would have been in agony.

Now, inexorably, came the final hours.

On New Year's Eve the nurses brought in a Chinese take-away – with some for me! There were male and female nurses and I thought they were the nearest things to angels on this earth. A group of them gathered with me in Dick's room trying to hold together some threads of normality.

Seeing the Old Year out was like seeing part of my life disappear and in my heart I feared Dick's life was ebbing with it.

A phone call came through – from Diana Dors. Dick had taken me to parties at her house on several occasions and I had grown to love her warm, funny personality.

'Is there anything you want, darling?'

'No, but thank you so much. We're getting through—'

'But what are you doing about food?'

'Well, Dick can't eat at the moment, and I am not really in the mood either.' True. I had lost half a stone in a week. 'The Press have camped at reception, which I have to pass to get to the cafeteria, so I don't bother.'

Diana said firmly: 'We can't have that.' And next day, her chauffeur arrived with a huge basket of fruit and biscuits. 'Courtesy of Miss Dors, ma'am. She hopes Mr Emery gets better.' Diana was such a kind and loving person. Only close friends knew about Dick's illness, as all this time I had been trying to stop the world from finding out just how ill Dick was. If he had got better, and wanted to work again, it certainly wouldn't help to have people thinking he was in poor health. So he made me swear I would tell everyone that he was suffering from gout!

'If anyone wants to know, just tell them I've got gout,' he told me, as his illness took hold. 'Promise?' And of course I did.

So that was the story I gave out to the reporters, the most important of whom was the gentleman from the Press Association, which services every national and regional newspaper in Britain.

When people opened their papers next morning they read: 'Dick Emery is suffering from gout', according to his lover, Fay Hillier.

Actually, Dick did suffer from gout. His big toes used to play him up like mad and anyone who has been through the same torment will know that it's not funny at all – whatever those old Charlie Chaplin movies may lead you to believe.

Up until then I had been trying to stay optimistic, making plans about how I would manage when I took Dick home. I said to one of the doctors: 'When I get him back, will I be able to cope with his medication on my own?'

The doctor looked at me sadly. 'I'm sorry,' he said. 'But I shouldn't count on being able to take him home.'

In that moment, for the first time, it dawned on me that I really was going to lose Dick for good. When I knew that he was finally succumbing, I asked someone to phone Josephine. She hadn't been to visit him and I was concerned that she might not know how seriously ill he was, although I had asked the hospital to keep her informed. At the time she was playing in a musical in Edinburgh. A couple of weeks earlier when he could still talk, he had spoken briefly to her but had tried to make light of his situation.

Josephine did come down, and I thought it only fair that she should have time alone with Dick, so when she arrived I moved out into the waiting room down the corridor. I asked a nurse to give her a message: 'I'll stay out for two hours, but after that I'm afraid I'll have to come back.' Two hours seemed so long I could hardly wait, but when I returned Josephine was still there. We didn't speak, but kept watch together on either side of Dick's bed, where we were joined by his children and Margaret Thomas. None of us could halt the tears that ran down our cheeks.

The vicar of Deptford, Canon David Diamond, arrived unexpectedly. He was a wonderful friend and even though Dick wasn't particularly religious, he said prayers around the bed, which did seem to calm us all.

Josephine had her family waiting and had to leave for a lunch date with them. The rest of us stayed. In the next hours the doctors took Dick off the ventilating machine and hand pumped his breathing to keep it going. 'Being sympathetic with his body,' was the term they used. But it didn't work.

'He's going, I'm afraid,' said a nurse.

The final moments were like something out of a TV hospital drama. The sorrow was real enough, but the action had a nightmarish quality. There really was a screen with a little *blip-blip* getting less and less until suddenly there was just one continuous tone accompanied by a horrible buzzing noise and I knew that was the end.

Only it wasn't.

They put electric pads on his chest and tried to restart his heart, which is normal procedure, but dreadful to witness.

It was then that I lost control. I'm ashamed to say I became hysterical. Dick had made me promise that I wouldn't let him be kept alive by machine but that's just what had been happening for the last few days and I couldn't do anything about it.

Now, I thought they were hurting him and it was more than I could stand. I was forcibly removed – gently but firmly, as they say – and taken to the waiting room.

Dick died on 3 January 1983. Exactly four years to the day after we met. When I was allowed back into the ward, every wire had been removed, the bed freshly smoothed and Dick looked as I wanted to remember him, his face peaceful, all the agony and torment gone.

No one else was in the room. Just Dick and me. I leant over and gathered him into my arms. He was warm and I cradled him for over an hour. For some reason I felt I had to help his soul on its way, to make up for all the terrible things that had happened to him that I hadn't been able to prevent.

'You're safe now, my darling,' I whispered to him. 'It's over – the pain and anguish are all gone. You're free, nothing can hurt you any more.'

I found that I wasn't thinking only of the last few dreadful weeks, but of his whole life, which was so beset by insecurities, guilt and disappointments.

Eventually, a doctor put his head round the door. 'It's time to go now,' he said gently.

They smuggled me out by a rear exit so that I wouldn't have to face the cameras and the questions, and I stayed the night with Margaret at her home.

After all that, the thing I wanted most was a long hot bath. I lay in it for hours, washing away the smell of the hospital and the trauma of the past endless days.

Then I slept the clock round. I dared not wake up for fear of what lay ahead. Trying to live when Dick had died seemed impossible. And this time he couldn't come back.

24. Afterwards

'Still getting laughs'

FAY

If only Dick had known how much he was loved, not just by women but by his millions of fans and even his fellow actors. If he had known the genuine respect they felt for his acting ability it might have gone a long way in giving him the confidence he lacked. But as is so often the case, by the time I received all these wonderful tributes it was too late for Dick to see them.

It's sad to think that many of the people who paid tribute to Dick have themselves now gone. But their tributes remain, and Dick would have been amused, proud and very pleased, and as no one has ever seen them, I'm including them here.

Roy Kinnear said 'I know that, now he's up there, the Great Editor in the sky is going to have to ask for a great many retakes as Dick starts making them all 'break up'. Miss you, Dick.'

Les Dawson told me 'I first met Dick Emery in Bournemouth which, as everybody knows, is a sort of Blackpool with 'O' Levels. Although a small man, he acted taller. One was never conscious of physical size, there was an air of confidence and dignity that transcended the aspect of the man. Show business is poorer by his passing.'

Eric Morecambe testified 'I was a great admirer. Dick had enormous talent and will not be replaced in his particular field of comedy. What a tragic loss.'

And June Whitfield declared 'I was very fond of Dick and will miss him as much as his many fans. His death is a great loss to the world of comedy and I always enjoyed working with him.'

To Bert Weedon he was talented, comical, enthusiastic, full of life and a good mate. He said he wouldn't mind betting that Dick would have conned some angel into giving him harp lessons!

Michael Bentine said that he had a million laughs with Dick and would never forget him, while Clive Dunn reminded me that when things got absolutely awful, Dick and he would always start to giggle – having a similar sense of tragedy.

What Ronnie Barker said was particularly touching. And Dick himself would have been gratified to hear it too. 'I admired Dick's skill and technique for many years. He was truly an actor's comedian and I never ceased to be amazed at the clarity and definition of his characters. Above all they were really funny. God bless him for that. In our memories may his Lampwick never burn him!'

From Spike Milligan: 'Dick? He was a strange but basically lovable person. And Lionel Jeffries hardly had to say that they loved every moment of each other's company – through laughter.

Charlie Drake was philosophical: 'For Dick, the stage was living. Whatever happened before or after was just waiting.'

Bill Cotton Jnr, 'Mr BBC LE', as I suppose he could be known, summed it all up. ' Dick laughed, loved and gave generously of himself to many people. Those who loved him will miss him but remember him with a smile. As Mandy might say: "You weren't half awful – but we liked you!"

Dick's funeral had the same unreal quality as his death in the hospital. For me it passed in a haze of misery. We now had full media attention. As well as the Press there were TV cameras only inches from our tear-stained faces. I had the distinct impression of being trapped in a tacky B-movie, with no hope of escape.

In the empty days after Dick died, Margaret gave her usual invaluable help with making arrangements for the funeral. Although even she couldn't help the atmosphere in the chapel at Mortlake Crematorium. With Josephine on one side of the coffin and me on the other, the natural chill turned frigid. Family, friends and familiar celebrity faces filled the pews. All I can remember is the absolute despair I felt, as after the service and a simple blessing, Dick's coffin moved with a purring sound over the runners, through the little curtains and out of sight into the furnace.

If it hadn't been for the support of Eileen and Lionel Jeffries, two of

Dick's closest friends to the end, I would have collapsed. They literally held me up and eventually helped me outside to see the wonderful carpet of flowers, sent from all over the world, in a last affectionate tribute to Dick.

You might think that was the end of it, but of course with Dick, nothing was ever that simple.

A few days later the Crematorium gave me Dick's ashes. I made a little shrine in my sitting room with his photo, some flowers, a candle and the ashes. It was comforting to have him home again. And there he stayed for several months. Every evening, I lit the candle and felt that he was with me.

One day, out of the blue, I received a phone call from my solicitor to say that I had to hand over Dick's ashes to Josephine. As their divorce had not gone through before he died, she was officially the widow and therefore entitled to his ashes.

What's more, they were going to be collected at twelve noon that day. I looked at my watch. It was 11.30. I panicked. What could I do? I couldn't bear to give up the last bit of Dick. But supposedly I had to, by law. I grabbed the urn and ran into the kitchen. Tears were pouring down my face, and I was sobbing and talking to myself in near hysteria. I opened the urn, which I had never done up to that point. Looking fearfully inside, I found dry grey granules. It actually looked like cat litter and for one mad moment I considered swapping it, but thought better of that. I decided instead to take out a tiny amount to keep for myself.

I was crying and shaking so much that I couldn't see round the kitchen, and couldn't find anything in which to put the ashes.

Time was running out. I spotted an empty coffee jar and, using a tablespoon, I carefully lifted out some granules. The whole thing was so pathetically macabre that I was beside myself with grief. Suddenly, I remembered Dick's humour. To this day I'm sure I heard him say: 'So now you've got me in a coffee jar,' followed by his wheezy chuckle. My tears stopped and I had an amazing sense of well-being.

The doorbell rang at the exact moment I closed the lid on the urn. Two unsmiling men dressed in black were waiting to take away Dick's ashes. Although bedraggled and tear-stained, I managed to hand them over with some dignity.

A few weeks after Dick's funeral, we had a memorial service for him, at St Paul's in Covent Garden. The actors' church. So many people, including Danny La Rue and June Whitfield, wanted to pay their respects. They travelled from all over, even overseas.

Dick would have been touched, especially by the presence of his eldest son Gill. I flew him in from America so he could say goodbye to the father he loved, but with whom he had spent so little time. Gill stayed with me and my children in Shepperton, where Dick's other children, Nick, Michael and Eliza, visited us. It was a loving happy reunion, even though inspired by a sad event.

St Paul's Church was so full that some people had to stand outside to hear the service. We tried to put the sadness behind us and make a celebration of Dick's life. Michael read a touching poem he had written on behalf of all Dick's children. There was singing and readings, and Bill Cotton gave a spirited tribute.

Unfortunately, Josephine felt she couldn't attend. But Victoria, Dick's fourth wife, did come. Iris his third wife had died, while Zelda and Irene had simply vanished from Dick's life. All his children were there, other family members, many celebrity colleagues and lifelong friends. Dozens of fans and who knows how many old flames. Dick certainly had a good send-off.

But even then we hadn't reached the end. Almost a year later, after endless discussions between our lawyers, Josephine took me to court over Dick's will. This much-publicized battle between us dragged poor Dick's name through the papers yet again. During his lifetime, Dick had a good relationship with the Press. He usually gave them a story, as he said: 'They'll print something anyway, so they might as well get it from the horse's mouth!'

That was fine if they were reporting on his work or some light-hearted affair. But haggling over his estate in public didn't appeal to me at all. To avoid going to court, I made Josephine what I thought was a reasonable offer, but she felt unable to accept. So we ended up in the courtroom making public what should have remained private.

For me, the most moving moment was when my counsel read out a letter that he used as an example of how much Dick loved me. It was one he wrote to me when he had left and was wanting to return for the last time.

And now I am alone. Nothing to distract me. Just me alone and the deep sense that you were once here. Your perfume is in the air.

How do I start to tell you why, why, why? Why do I set out to destroy something so beautiful, so precious? Is it some kind of madness? Please God, no. What kind of madness is it that makes me think I can do without you? That as soon as I've severed myself from you I am like a frightened child alone in the dark.

How dear you are to me is almost impossible to put into words and yet I do this terrible thing to you. That you even speak to me is a miracle.

I've been looking at the movies, which we took in Australia. All those wonderful things we did together. You look so lovely as you walk past the camera. I look at you and you fulfil every desire that is in me. Your every little movement pulls at my heartstrings.

Could I find it possible to live without you?

Beloved, I'd rather die. For when you're not there I don't exist, a shadow takes my place and I am empty and devoid of any feeling.

One day I will kneel at your feet and ask your forgiveness. Pray God you will find it in yourself to do so.

My only desire now is to make you happy again, with no shadows this time lurking behind those lovely eyes of yours. I want to see those lines of anxiety disappear. I want to make you feel whole again, a woman again, my woman, my beloved woman, my own Fay.

May God forgive me for what I have done.

I love you so.

DICK

Eventually, the judge awarded Josephine less than I had offered, so we endured four days in the High Court and wasted a lot of Dick's money for nothing. I wonder if he would have been amused or appalled that his women were still fighting over him so long after he had gone?

That at last was the end. The dust settled. The Press finally lost interest and we were left to get on with our lives as best we could.

The last place where Dick and I worked before his final illness and death was in the Devonshire Park Theatre, Eastbourne, a grand old place that has staged pantomimes, plays and summer shows as far back as people can remember.

I had been with him during the recording in front of a live audience of the BBC's *Spotlight on Dick Emery*, the story of his life. In fact he was really ill at the time and the programme was never shown.

Three years later I was back on that stage in the summer run of the hilarious farce *Pyjama Tops*, which starred John Inman. I had met John in New Zealand six years earlier, when Dick and I were staying at the same hotel as him. They were old friends and John remembers the occasion.

'I was sunbathing next to the swimming pool; it was very peaceful and I was hoping not to be disturbed. Suddenly I heard these clicking footsteps approaching, and squinting through the sun, I saw what looked like a real "old queen" mincing towards me. Oh hell, I thought, now I'll be trapped for hours. Just then the "old queen" gave his famous "cod trip" and I realized it was Dick Emery. What a relief. He was so convincing he really had me going!'

A few months after Dick died, John asked me if I would like to work with him for his summer season. But I was still grieving and couldn't get myself together. The next year John gave me what one almost never gets in show business. A second chance. By then I had recovered enough to enjoy that and many more very happy seasons with him.

But on this opening night in Eastbourne it was impossible for my thoughts not to drift back to the last time I had set foot there with Dick.

As I sat at my dressing table, something moved in the air behind me and I caught a swift fluttering of a small winged insect. I turned, startled, and I saw a beautiful butterfly swoop low past my shoulder and up again to the ceiling.

Its wings were brown, speckled with white, and it bobbed around in a kind of joyful freedom that was quite captivating before it settled on the top of my make-up mirror, close to the naked bulbs but seemingly quite undaunted by the light or the heat.

I don't think it is generally known, but in the theatre there's a legend that a butterfly is the spirit of a dead actor or performer. Call it myth, tradition or even superstition. All I know is that my dressing room had no windows, my door was shut and that butterfly had already caused uproar by upstaging John Inman and Maurice Thorogood a few minutes before.

I had nine entrances and eight changes of costume during the play, so it wasn't until the interval that Maurice poked his head round the door.

'You feeling okay?' he said, staring at me closely.

I nodded, then gestured up at the top of the mirror. 'Look!'

'Good God,' he said. 'It's amazing. That butterfly has just given us ten minutes of business on the stage. We got so many laughs you wouldn't believe it.'

'What do you mean?' I asked.

'Well, it just wouldn't go away. It was fluttering down on our heads, dive-bombing us and circling around. Of course John milked it for all he was worth! He flapped at it and talked to it and people were just falling about laughing. It was the butterfly getting the laughs.'

I could believe it. John is always ready for anything that happens. If somebody sneezes or a baby cries or someone drops something – he can ad-lib and get a laugh out of it. He's quite brilliant at it.

'It's amazing,' Maurice said, staring at the small brown and white visitor. 'To come up here and find it's in your dressing room makes the hairs stand up on the back of my neck!'

I didn't know whether to laugh or cry. When Maurice had gone I whispered: 'Dick, are you there? Is that you still getting laughs?'

A poem that Reverend David Diamond read out at Dick's funeral seemed very apt at that moment:

> Though I am dead, grieve not for me with tears
> Think not of death with sorrowing and fears
> I am so near that every tear you shed
> Touches and tortures me though you think me dead
> But when you laugh and sing with glad delight
> My soul is lifted upward to the light
> Laugh and be glad for all that life is giving
> And I, though dead, will share your joy in living.

I don't regret a second of the time I spent with Dick. Good times or bad. Four years was not long enough and I wish we had had more time.

For all his insecurities, I like to think that Dick had found peace at last and that we would have stayed together. But who knows?

Only one thing is certain. In the end I was the only woman in his life he didn't leave on purpose.

That helps a lot.

Dick always ended his act with this song written for him by Eric Winston:

> The time has come
> To say, my friends
> This is where
> The evening ends
> And if you've enjoyed the show
> May I say before you go
> Remember me, the real . . .
> Dick Emery.

Career Highlights

1932   Enters talent contest at the Grange Cinema, Kilburn – and wins.

1933   First professional engagement: singing and dancing with the Silver Songsters at Walthamstow Palace, followed by tours.

1934   One-night appearances in variety theatres around the country.

1935–8   Trains as baritone under Signor Cecco Mattannia.

1940   Sings in stage musical *Land of Smiles*, also understudying Richard Tauber.

1941   Chorus line in *The Merry Widow*, London.

1942–6   The Gang Show, Ralph Reader's wartime entertainment group.

1946   Summer variety show, Grand Theatre, Brighton.
Tours music halls around Britain.
Ugly Sister in pantomime *Cinderella*, Blackpool.

1946–78   Pantomimes every year.

1946–79   Summer shows every year.

1947   Windmill Theatre, London.

1948   PANTOMIME: *Cinderella*, Liverpool.
Start of regular appearances in BBC radio shows, including *Show Time, Variety Bandbox, ITMA, Henry Hall's Guest Night, Music Hall, Happy-go-Lucky, Spring Salad, Summer Showtime, Workers' Playtime*.

1949   *Variety season*: Poplar Civic Theatre.

1950   Summer show, Winter Gardens, Isle of Wight.

1951–6   TV: including *Up Spirits, Kaleidoscope, Fast and Loose, The*

Spice of Life, Jon Pertwee Show, Max Wall Show. RADIO: *The Goon Show.*

1952   Bognor summer show: *Dazzle.*
1954   Season at Chiswick Empire.
        Variety tour, UK.
1955   Season at Adelphi Theatre, Strand.
1956–9 RADIO: *Educating Archie.*
1960   Tours with stage comedy *Don't Shoot, We're English!*
        TV: Ted Ray Show. RADIO: *Funny Side Up, London Lights, It's a Fair Cop, Variety Playhouse.* FILMS: *The Mukkinese Battle Horn* (The Goons), *Light Up the Sky.*
1961   TV SERIES: *It's a Square World.*
1962   FILMS: *Mrs Gibbons' Boys, The Wrong Arm of the Law.*
        PANTOMIME: *Puss in Boots* (Kibdib Palladium).
1963   RADIO: fourteen appearances in various comedy shows.
1963–81 BBC TV: *The Dick Emery Show.*
1965   FILMS: *The Big Job, The Intelligence Men, The Knack.*
1966   FILM: *The Wrong Box.* PANTOMIME: *Mother Goose,* Cardiff.
1967   First tour of Australia.
        PANTOMIME: *Cinderella,* Streatham, South London.
1969   Australia, records six *Dick Emery Shows* for Australian TV viewers.
1970   *Desert Island Discs,* with Roy Plomley.
        Royal Variety Show.
        PANTOMIME: *Dick Whittington,* Leeds.
1970   First album: *Dick Emery Sings.*
1970–80 Various BBC TV appearances, including *Comedy Playhouse, The Great Quilow, The Good Old Days, Seven Faces of J.D., Wednesday Magazine, Play Your Hunch, The Singing Summers.*
1971   Australian tour.
        Single 'If You Love Her' makes the Top Twenty in the UK.
1972   Howard and Wyndham Theatre tour, UK.
        FILM: *Ooh, You Are Awful!*
1974   PANTOMIME: *Goldilocks and the Three Bears,* Wimbledon.
1975   Australia and New Zealand tour. TV commercials.

1977   FILM: *Find the Lady*.
UK variety tour.

1979   *Dick Emery's Cookbook* published. Australia and New
Zealand tour.

1980   BBC TV series: *Legacy of a Murder*.
Australia and New Zealand tour.

1981   BBC TV series: *Jack of Diamonds*. Australia and New
Zealand tour.

1982   TV: *Comedy of Errors*.

Index